"The Truth"

## Other books by Sam Pickering

### Essay Collections
*A Continuing Education*
*The Right Distance*
*May Days*
*Still Life*
*Let It Ride*
*Trespassing*
*The Blue Caterpillar*
*Living to Prowl*
*Deprived of Unhappiness*
*A Little Fling*
*The Last Book*
*The Best of Pickering*
*Indian Summer*
*Autumn Spring*
*Journeys*
*Dreamtime*
*The Splendour Falls*
*All My Days Are Saturdays*
*Happy Vagrancy*
*One Grand, Sweet Song*
*Parade's End*
*The World Was My Garden, Too*
*Terrible Sanity*
*The Gate in the Garden Wall*

### Travel
*Walkabout Year*
*Waltzing the Magpies*
*Edinburgh Days*
*A Tramp's Wallet*

### Literary Studies
*The Moral Tradition in English Fiction, 1785-1850*
*John Locke and Children's Books in Eighteenth-Century England*
*Moral Instruction and Fiction for Children, 1749-1820*

### Teaching
*Letters to a Teacher*

### Memoir
*A Comfortable Boy*

# "The Truth"

Sam Pickering

Lake Dallas, Texas

FIRST EDITION

Requests for permission to reprint material
from this work should be sent to:

Permissions
Madville Publishing
P.O. Box 358
Lake Dallas, TX 75065

Author Photograph: Eliza Pickering
Cover Design: Kimberly Davis
Cover image: "The Piper of Dreams" by Estella Louisa
Michaela Canziani (1887-1964)


ISBN: 978-1-956440-27-0 Paperback,
ISBN: 978-1-956440-28-7 Ebook
Library of Congress Control Number: 2023937237

## Dedication

I have dedicated most of my books to Vicki. Without her I wouldn't be "me." But amid the pages and the briar patches of words she often vanishes, and I regret that. She is a wife and mother, a person akin to the ideal woman Wordsworth described as "bright with something of angelic light." Yet she is a heck of a lot more. On her dresser is a voodoo doll. It's not a New Orleans or Port-au-Prince doll, but a Storrs doll, domesticated and rectangular, five inches wide and six tall, a pocket recycled from a gray soiled apron. Sketched on each side of the pocket is a box-shaped man with stick arms and legs, topped by a square head. Along the ribs of one man appears the name Putin, on the other Trump. Every morning Vicki sticks two hairpins into each figure. "You can't predict what'll happen," she says. I think chicken feet would be more effective than hairpins or since this is New England maybe vegan wishbones made out of gluten and tofu. But then the doll is Vicki's, not mine, as in truth this and my other books are hers, too. So, for the last time let me write, "For Vicki, with love."

# Table of Contents

# And So It Goes

Last Thursday I mailed the revised manuscript of my final book to a press. My writing years had been long and good, "albeit unexpected," I wrote Mike a college classmate. "I intend to sit in a chair at the edge of the driveway and on sunny days doze through hours waking up occasionally to identify birds on the feeder. My hands and lap will be empty, and I won't worry about wind scattering papers across the yard." On Tuesday Mike answered my note. "Given all the books you have written, it makes me sad to hear that you have written your last book. Please remember what mighty things 80-year-olds can still do. For instance, Goethe taught himself Greek when he was 80. Too bad he died at 81."

"What a good first paragraph for an essay," I thought as I read Mike's letter. "But I have moved on," I told Vicki later. "Maybe," Vicki said, "but you are still sitting in your study and haven't migrated to the drive. Before you hop over the blank wall at the end of your days, you'll pull a pencil out of your long white robe and scribble something on the bricks. You will never be pencil-less. Friends will supply you with writing material long after they move into condos in Skeleton Park." Vicki was right. The next week, Bob, an academic friend, wrote me. He said that I "owed it to the profession" to write a book describing my graduate school years at Princeton. "It would delight. You had so much fun." I "loved" graduate school. The years were rich with books and colorful anecdotes. Nevertheless I demurred. "I knew too many people too well," I told Bob. The decent autobiographer fabricates place and characters. He fences his pages and refuses to let actual people cross the margins, even if Time has transformed them into pale revenants.

I didn't want to disappoint Bob so I let him down with an anecdote, asking if he recalled Sue Jernigan. Sue was a mathematician and left graduate school after two years. She did not make a strong impression, so to jog Bob's memory I described Sue in some detail. She was short and "a little dumpy," I wrote. Her hair was black and curly, and the curls were plastered so tightly against her forehead they looked like fiddleheads. Even on hot days she wore calf-high white plastic boots. After abandoning graduate studies, she became a CPA, eventually rising to "head financial honcho" of a company that manufactured dental tools, items like scalers and picks, mouth mirrors and saliva ejectors. Sue didn't marry and died at sixty-five. She invested her money with mathematical precision and was well heeled. Four years ago on a cruise in the Caribbean I met her niece and heir.

"On every island," the woman told me, "I drink a Mojito or three in memory of Aunty Sue. Her money made this cruise possible. As soon as her big bucks appeared in my bank account, I stopped teaching 2nd grade, sold my bungalow, and started traveling practically living on cruise ships." "I loved Aunty and I'm grateful to her," the woman added after a good snort, "and I always leave a heeltap at the bottom of my glass just in case she's thirsty and is hanging around out of sight." Bob answered my letter. He said that despite "the plethora of details," he wasn't sure he remembered Sue. He asked if she'd been an undergraduate at Long Island University. Sue and her boozy niece were fabrications. I'm glad Bob didn't remember her. If he had, he would clearly have been on the way to Ga-Ga Land.

No matter how writers struggle to type "The End" on last books, many are doomed to fail. Life does not stop hammering raw hours into anecdotes. Recently I had my eyes tested. The optometrist was experienced and competent. She was also garrulous and sensible. Halfway down the scroll of my medications, she paused and said, "Lupron. My father took that after the doctor removed his prostate. How do you take it?" "A shot," I said. "Where do you get the shot?" she asked. "In my behind," I answered. "Father got his in the stomach," she replied, "but they didn't do any good. The cancer went to his brain, and he passed." "I'm sorry," I said. "Don't be," she said. "The last year of his life was terrible, and it's good he's gone. I don't know where he is, but any time or place would be better than here and now." "What did you say then?" Vicki asked when I described the examination. "I didn't say anything. I just kept staring into the phoropter."

Like strangers, friends endlessly mold the clay of unplanned hours into anecdotes. Shortly after I replied to Bob, Savely wrote me. Savely taught botany at a college in Ohio for forty years. He retired the same year I retired. Instead of continuing to explore wood and field, he hibernated. As a result, dealing with ordinary academic things gradually became almost impossible. "Sam," he began, "last week I received an email from a former student." "You are a treasure to this world," Savely's old student wrote, "and every time I think about what you taught me about life and trees, I smile and am thankful. I will never forget you." "Sam, throughout my career I prided myself on honesty," Savely wrote, "but I don't have any idea who this man was or is. Must I tell him that I have completely forgotten him? You've written books. Tell me what to say to him." The most important skill a teacher should have is the ability to lie convincingly. Decency, compassion, and ease of living rest on the necessity of lying. Before entering a classroom, every beginning teacher should purchase a box of crayons, the biggest one containing 120 different colors. He should use these to color truths making them acceptable and kindly, transforming them into life-enhancing lies. "Students are children, and adults who write their old teachers have regressed and are momentarily children again," I wrote Savely. "Thank your correspondent profusely. Tell him, and use my words, that his letter 'meant the world' to you. Say that you'd forgotten how much you adored teaching until you received his letter. Tell him his words brought tears to your eyes. End by assuring him that 'of course' you remember him and 'with great affection and admiration.'"

"It's a wonder you didn't advise Savely to fill an eyedropper with water and sprinkle false tears on his reply," Vicki said. To be truthful, I considered doing so, but what's appropriate for me would have been too much for Savely, and I had already elbowed him a long way out of his comfort zone. At dinner that night Vicki asked if I remembered the song "Heartaches by the Number" in which the singer lamented having troubles by the score. Friends, she said, won't let you disappear into silence. They'll ask for advice, urge you to write more books, and you will oblige them. She said I resembled the monk in the old story who was addicted to chess. When a bald-headed angel asked what he'd do on learning that a meteor was hurtling through the sky and would destroy the earth in five minutes, the monk replied, "I'd move my bishop to D-5." "Why a bald-headed angel?" I asked. "That's for you to figure out on the page," Vicki said. "Forget the dark ages at Princeton. Let your light shine in the present and write a book compounded out of equal portions of self-help and fiddle-faddle."

I mulled Vicki's suggestion for a couple of days. It was intriguing and seductive. Giving advice is easier than receiving it. For my part I have rarely paid attention to unsolicited advice. I think most advice presumptuous and more irritating than poison ivy even when applied with a slather of lubricating words. Only when caught in the tightening coils of the prolegomenon to a tedious didactic lecture have I asked advice. I did so not to learn but to force concision upon the speaker and end the conversation. "What do you think is the best course of action? Put it in a nutshell," I say. The metaphor of the nut is apt if applied to my conversationalist, but only the Great Grammarian Above can excuse the puerility of "best course of action." Being opinionated is a sign of inflexibility and intellectual senility, and I avoid the company of people who look into the dark and see clearly. Often they are middle-aged, financially successful, and too arrogantly self-satisfied to ponder. A few have begun to be fearful. To study one's life and discover that he is a fool like other men whom he has learned to despise is rarely pleasant. On the other hand, certainly, no one should listen to advice from young people, if indeed the youthful are people. As for the old, they find their own council wanting. Life has taught them that the most efficacious way to avoid being tarred by the misfortunes of others is to eschew giving advice. The old are the center of their lives and usually are indifferent to the missteps of others, including, and especially, those of family members.

Open season on the simple and wide-eyed never shuts down, and professional advice-givers are always on the hunt. Few are disinterested. Not all are honorable and many are more intent on balancing their finances than stabilizing the lives of others. Among some groups of advice-givers, politicians, for example, corruption is rife and integrity endangered. Almost always their advice leads to enervating skepticism and the dissolution of the hope to believe. The throats of people panhandling advice are, as Romans recounts, open sepulchers. "With their tongues they have used deceit" and "the venom of asps is under their lips." Paul put his advice a little strongly for contemporary latitudinarian taste. It would be congenial if the p were deleted from asps and es added to form the plural. Among William Hazlitt's essays is "On the Ignorance of the Learned." In many cases learning, he wrote, was "a foil to common sense" and "a substitute for true knowledge." Books, he argued, "are less often made use of as 'spectacles' to look at nature with, than as blinds to keep out its strong light and shifting scenery from weak eyes and indolent dispositions." Of more danger to people seeking advice is the "Ignorance of the Ignorant." Alas, people thirsting after advice are often indiscriminate and are influenced by enthusiasm and noisy advertisements more than by tranquil reason. To emend the lesion-worn maxim: you can steer a mule away from water but he will return and drink. Complicating matters is that what passes for salubrious advice in the morning may appear deleterious in the evening. Moreover, as Francis Bacon remarked, "he that talketh what he knoweth, will also talk what he knoweth not."

To become a guru necessitates reducing complexity to simplicity. To calloused oldsters whose energy is flagging, simplicity is more alluring than complexity. But writing a book on advice would require anorexic paring beyond my dietary capacity. Often the injurious, as well as the beneficial, effects of advice are not in words themselves but are imbedded in the characters of the people who receive the advice. How does the author of a book on advice deal with the unamenable but heart-felt imprecation suggesting that someone's behavior is so improper that he should take The Blue Flame Special to Hades? All lives are patchworks of deeds and thoughts. Should the author of an advice book impose a misleading narrative consistency on his life? How responsible should he think himself for injurious actions ostensibly taken by his readers?

Formatting a satisfactory book would be onerous. It would have to include passages from famous practitioners, quotations from literati like the aforementioned Francis Bacon and, to balance the genders, from Agnes Repplier. Much of their advice would not be in the form of imperatives but in statements functioning as signs directing the alert, for example, Repplier's observation, "There is no illusion so permanent as that which enables us to look backward with complacency" or perhaps her judgement, "A man destitute of humor is apt to be a formidable person, not subject to sudden deviations from his chosen path, and incapable of frittering away his elementary forces by pottering over both sides of a question. He is often to be respected, sometimes to be feared, and always—if possible—to be avoided." I wouldn't want to know what Vicki thought if I quoted Myrtle Reed's statement, "Marriage appears to be somewhat like a grape. People swallow a great deal of indifferent good for the sake of the lurking bit of sweetness and never know until it is too late whether the venture was wise."

Indeed, some people offering advice are to be feared. They are zealots, fiery enthusiasts punishing dissenters and intent on creating battalions of goose-stepping disciples. When Moses came down from Mt. Sinai after bivouacking in a cloud for forty days and nights, he carried the stony pages of his advice book, carved under the pseudonym Yahweh. On reaching the camp of the Israelites, he discovered that many of his followers had drifted from his aegis and begun to worship a golden calf. He threw his pages to the ground, shattering them, then burned the calf, ground it into powder, and mixing the ashes in water, forced the Israelites to drink it. There is no ire like that of a forsaken advice guru. Next he enlisted the Sons of Levi who had not worshipped the calf and instructed them to "put every man his sword by his side, and go in and out from gate to gate throughout the camp, and slay every man his brother, and every man his companion, and every man his neighbor." The "children of Levi" were faithful servants and killed "that day about three thousand men."

Throughout history theocratic advice has led to blood. In the name of sanity and benevolence—soft-eyed Jersey and Guernsey calves--I'd exclude such advice from my book. Unfortunately the best laid attempts often go astray, and thoughtful intentions frequently lead to evil. The ardor for reformation and uplift has condemned countless people to the stake. It has burned libraries and art galleries, smashed sculptures, salted fields, and blasted cities. It has erased Time's past, present, and future hours. Although no description of man's bestial behavior would appear on my pages, a superior book must include advice proffered by life's higher animals, a prime example being the words of The Three Macaques, "see no evil, hear no evil, speak no evil." In an age addicted to inclusion, quoting learned monkeys might arouse the jealousy of the lower animals and force me to cite the Innumerable Sons of Bitches in North Georgia and the Texas legislature with its Dens of Rattlesnakes in the Sand.

Having endured much tinkering recently, the advice I can give is medical. I am up to the moment on many procedures. Unfortunately television medicine provides many older people with all their medical knowledge. Instead of consulting doctors, they consult advertisements, many of the products sounding automotive: Warfarin, a mid-sized Ford pickup, the right taillight shattered, the paint in its cargo bed scoured by hay, the flakes burned off by manure, and the front bumper dangling and tilting practically scraping the ground. In contrast Xarelto seems a Chevrolet sports car, deceptively red and flashy, but inexpensive and loud on the highway, appealing to unformed youth and to adults who are not-quite quite. Synthroid is a semi-trailer truck, its tractor massive and its trailer so long that it appears to curve—the kind of truck that travels the frozen highways of Alaska and British Columbia in winter and is forever sliding and tipping and becoming the star of "Ice Road Truckers."

"You are not your own best doctor," Vicki has long told me. When she learned I was seriously pondering writing the advice book, she warned me against making suggestions about iatric matters, "that is, if you want to keep ambulance-chasing lawyers away from our bank account. Like the jejunum, hospital corridors are winding and confusing, and you might steer a rotund man into the wrong operating theater causing him to have a cesarean section rather than a hemorrhoidectomy." In this country, there are four lawyers for every lunatic, she warned, "and you won't be able to avoid being sued." However, to suggest removing a corn on a big toe by roasting a black snail was all right, she said. "After the snail is well-done, sprinkle it with cardamum, and wrap it in a white cloth. Once the snail cools, place it firmly on the corn and plaster it over with moleskin. Do not remove the covering until the seventh day. Then the corn will be gone. Under no circumstances, however, prescribe cures for ailments above the talus."

As usual Vicki was graphic and right. I hadn't considered the dangers of giving medical advice with such surgical precision. As a result I've decided not to turn one of the chapters of the book into a waiting room. However, almost all the people who write me are of a certain age. They always ask about my wellbeing after which they describe their healths and those of family members and mutual friends. Parts of the letters are tally sheets, accounts of comings and goings, of who's up and who's down, and who's seesawing in-between. Thoughtful and descriptive, the letters contain much useful and interesting medical lore. Instead of advice which often takes the form of maxims sharp as scalpels, the writers ruminate. Because the ruminations slow my reading and make me ponder, I decided that if I wrote a book I'd include excerpts from their letters. The excerpts would not recommend medical procedures, but they would make readers think which is, of course, what good advice does.

The most recent letter I received was from my friend Dennis. His mother died in April. She had dementia and suffered from several debilitating diseases. "Her death," he wrote, "was more prolonged than death should be, thanks to the immaturity of the western world." His mother was, Dennis recalled, "a person who always had dreams of adventure-from skating at Rockefeller Center, becoming a singer during the tin pan alley days, and visiting her own mother's land in western Ireland." "None of those dreams ever came to pass;" he wrote, "yet, she was never bitter because of that. The dreaming seemed in some ways enough, and once the dementia settled in, she believed she actually did achieve some of the dreams on the list. I think we all live much more of our lives in our heads than we care to admit, even if those heads aren't quite as sure of the facts as they used to be." Dennis's statement was much, much better and deeper than a sheaf of epigrammatic pages of medical advice.

Frequently the soundest advice I know seems to be "put not your trust in men or institutions." Lives revolve in circles which at times seem endless. "Around and around in the same tedious groove," Vicki said, explaining why people unexpectedly jettisoned common sense and behaved irrationally. Although obviously unsound, some charlatans are so appealingly colorful and thus seductive that people consult them simply to break the tedium of everyday life. Doing so is risky. In the 1950s one of the most popular financial advisors in Tennessee was a man "whom no one in his right mind" should have consulted. Like the biographies of many successful people, the details of his early years are hazy. He may have gotten his start in Claiborne County fondling copperheads and drinking battery acid in church. Certainly he did not attribute his success to a university education. Former friends said his success stemmed from marrying a wealthy widow. She wasn't a peacharine, but her savings were sweet and juicy.

She was some years older, had been married to a prominent Holiness minister, and was quoted by a member of her Canasta claque as saying, "my husband thinks a person who believes in a god will swallow anything." Witness the recent agitation in North Georgia following a viewing of the stones extracted from the gall bladder of a centripetal, sanctified sister. The stones were bigger than most artifacts found in the biliary tract and were covered with scratches. Bertie the owner of the Smokin' Oak Pit examined the marks and said they were letters. When arranged "properly," Bertie said the stones spelled the ingredients of his special "Red Pepper Flakes" barbeque sauce. "Hogwash," a Holiness lexicographer exclaimed and said the marks were Aramaic. "When translated into God's own English, they spelled 'Praise the Holy Family and King Jesus the Divine Carpenter.'"

The peculiar exuberant doings of North Georgia aside, I think that advertising acumen not his wife's money was responsible for the financial advisor's success. His initial ads appeared in small town newspapers and attracted his first clients. When sincerity and decency are made of words, they are easy to counterfeit. He told potential clients that they'd "be treated like one of the family," an assurance that should have made folks grab their wallets and skedaddle. Once in his presence gulls found his personality so magnetic that until their money vanished they couldn't resist his advice. In the ad I saw, he sat behind a rolltop desk, its cubby holes nests of papers. On the top was a cigar box full of pens, pencils, and erasers. Next to it was a mantle clock that on the hour played "Dixie," on the half hour, "Sitting at the Feet of Jesus." Perched on the man's shoulder was Tree Frog his tame opossum. While Tree Frog's tail wrapped around his neck, the man leaned close to the opossum's head, the animal's pink nose almost touching his ear lobe. "I will make your fortune," the ad read, "I have sources others only imagine. Don't play dead. Wake up. Invest with me, and your money will roll over and growl." As the old maxim puts it, when fishing for fools, bait your hook with the promise of money.

After losing their savings, I suspect that not only did his investors growl but they also hissed and screeched. Would that a person could rely on advice promulgated by educational institutions. But they, too, carry opossums on their shoulders. Recently a university in New England, a "seat of higher learning," announced the expenditure of seventy million dollars to expand its amusement factory by building an ice hockey pavilion, containing a rink, the usual offices and dressing rooms, and an auditorium seating twenty-six hundred spectators. The project came wrapped in furry words like donations. Still, the tail was visible. Obviously the university valued entertainment and the publicity it garnered on sports pages more than schooling.

As cases of coronavirus dropped, another educational institution reopened an ice cream parlor but kept the library shut. A person could read the dedication atop an ice cream cake but not a page of a library book. My friend Josh wrote the library on behalf of an emeritus professor who taught at the school for more than forty years. The professor was an old-fashioned academic who explored libraries and country homes here and abroad. He unearthed neglected manuscripts and wrote several books and scores of articles. After his retirement, he went to the library every weekday. Always he was there when the doors opened at eight o'clock. He spent mornings in his carrel hidden in a keep of books, not leaving until he went home early in the afternoon. Each year he wrote additional articles, all of which appeared in good scholarly quarterlies. He was eighty-two years old and suffered badly from cancer. In great part, research was his life, and the library his second home. At the ebb of the virus after his friend received both vaccination shots, Josh sent his letter, telling me, "I'm ashamed I didn't write earlier." Josh urged the library to let his friend resume his studies "for scholarly and humanitarian reasons," noting that returning to the library would raise his friend's spirits and enrich his declining days. Josh stressed that he did not make the request for himself or anyone else or with his friend's knowledge. He said that "rules must always be malleable" and "that the best led academic lives were led both within and beyond rules." "Do you suppose the library will behave decently and admit him?" Josh asked me. "No," I said. "All those years devoted to the university, teaching and writing—won't they count for something?" "No," I repeated. I was right.

Rules are only guidelines and should be bent for decency and kindness. Sadly universities are no longer alma maters knowing their children one by one as Cardinal Newman wrote, but treadmills, in today's phraseology, unbending corporations, "businesses specializing in selling football and basketball," my friend Warner says. In the anonymity of institutions people lose individuality and become suits. Detaching from the inhumane becomes difficult, and averting one's eyes when barefoot Poverty limps pass treading on thorns becomes progressively easier and more comfortable. Insensible conformity ultimately wrecks character and if there is such a thing as a soul destroys it. "Are you going to suggest in your advice book that people should consult institutions rather than people?" Josh asked. "No," I said for the third time, "neither people nor institutions, and certainly not me."

I decided not to write a book. "To compose our character is our duty," Montaigne wrote, "not to compose books, and to win, not battles and provinces, but order and tranquility in our conduct. Our great and glorious masterpiece is to live appropriately." Often recognizing good advice is difficult, but when a person perceives it he should follow it. The pages I read in the spring were green and natural, maybe a little refined but not bleached or crazed with print. They pushed thoughts about writing another book aside and occupying my mind and sight satisfied me. Much was familiar, and I did not analyze. Days were garlanded, and I simply looked one moment at blossoms blanketing a Crimson Cloud cultivar of an English Hawthorne, the next at the small, sweet bristles of dwarf fothergilla. Wisteria dangled from the crowns of trees with the nonchalance of brides' maids. In the Beaver Pond, four Canada geese goslings fed on sedges and pond grass, their parents a moving bracket protecting them. Yellow Iris flourished in a marsh, and on Crimean linden the bark broke across the trunk in heavy surfer's waves creating deep troughs. "And the glowworm shines green in the midst of green leaves," I said, recalling a line from a forgotten summer song.

I was tranquil and forgot about the done and

undone. I watched a pileated woodpecker hammer into a rotten stump and a solitary vireo land on the birdbath in the side yard. Dovecotes of bugle spread across the backyard. The fox kits left the burrow in the wood behind the house and dispersed. For a few days one remained behind thick-coated and golden red. I fed it scraps and dog food until it, too, left. Shortly afterward, Uncle Old Man Possum one of Tree Frog's descendants explored the den. The ground outside the den looked like the entrance to the lair of a small ogre. Scattered atop the dirt raised around the opening were the leftovers of a turkey dinner, the skull of a groundhog, a fawn's leg, wings from a crow, and tails of rabbits and squirrels. The treasure was the "petrified" remains of a long dead fox. The fox had all its teeth. They were white and polished, and the skeleton was in one piece. Holding it together were dried ligaments and a wrap of black, leathery skin, odorless, furless, and taunt as the batter head of a snare drum. The dried juices of decay glued the skin to the skull, and the fox's mouth was open, grinning in a rictus and looking like a gargoyle on a medieval cathedral. I sawed through the fox's neck near the scapula and added the skull and attached link of spine to my remnant collection in the garage.

When catkins rained down from shagbark hickories, female snapping turtles began wandering, searching for the right soil in which to lay eggs. Star flowers rose out of leaf litter on dry woodsy slopes looking like white enameled antique jewelry. The fragrances of lilac, autumn olive, oriental bittersweet, and yellowwood transformed breezes into perfumeries and awakened my sense of smell from the long sleep caused by coronavirus. My life has never been and will never be a masterpiece, but it is okay, and if I were writing an advice book, I'd tell people to moderate their hopes and desires, to temper their opinions, and to revere the book of nature. Its pages turn every day. I'd also urge them to garden. Gardening, William Cobbett wrote, "tends to make home pleasant; and to endear to us the spot on which it is our lot to live." The peonies along my driveway no longer blossom, and this fall I plan to replace them with Iris. I've ordered several rhizomes and am eager to get them into the ground. The names of some are too poetic for my liking, among others, Mango Passion, Sunrise Elegy, Dancing on Air, and Butterscotch Kiss. I expect, however, they will adapt to my plebian ways, and once the car is in the garage, they and I will thrive and bloom. My last suggestion to people is that they eat a siddleberry sandwich. Until recently I'd never heard of siddleberrys, and I don't know what such a sandwich tastes like, but three nights ago in a dream I ate one. The next morning, I awoke refreshed and smiling. If a friend asks for advice, recommend that he try a sandwich. Discovering what a siddleberry is and trying to buy a quart of them in the local grocery should keep him busy for a while and take his mind off what's bothering him.

# On Again, On Again

During the past ten years, I have stopped writing a dozen times. In May I quit twice. The second pause lasted eleven days almost long enough to think, but not really believe, that I could free myself from scribentes morbus. I worked hard to distract myself. I mowed the grass when it didn't need it. I bought plants for the back stoop. Despite their being green slaves or at best indentured servants, I tried to make them comfortable. I put them in big pots with lots of branch and root room. I did not let them dry out, and I made sure they had nice places in the sun. I also talked to the trees around the house, most of which I'd known since they were saplings. I wished them happy summers and told them that I hoped their seeds would land in good fertile places. A few trees waved their new leaves. Sadly although they and I were linked in the web of life, they spoke an unfamiliar vocabulary, and I could not understand them.

I needed an intervention to break my addiction. I imagined Big Billy Goat Gruff lumbering into the study, hammering the Troll of Writing with his horns, trampling my pencil points with his hooves, and tossing all my writing paper into the drainage ditch running under the road in front of the house. Would that I could say a charm like the one that sent "the great ugly troll" downstream. "So snip, snap, snout, / This tale's told out." During the hard days of the coronavirus epidemic, many people purchased pets hoping that the animals would divert their attention from loneliness. Unfortunately, for me pets like pens are things I'd like to escape. For decades dogs have determined the course of my days. Wearing a dog collar has drained my energy and rubbed my moods raw. I am as tired of the pull and jerk of leashes as I am the wrench of words.

At day six, my withdrawal symptoms worsened. The hours I was free to do nothing weighed me down. Vicki prescribed television. The medicine did not take. Being stung by bees and wasps doesn't bother me, but shows delectating in crime and violence cause an anaphylactic reaction. Although news programs nauseated me, the one time I listened to a political harangue was surprisingly salutary as it reminded me that I'd neglected to get a shingles shot. "Try sports," my friend Josh suggested. Baseball occasions sleeping sickness. Basketball with chest bumps, fist pumps, and slam dunks seems a prequel to "Breaking Bad" while only Republicans watch football. Informed sports talk is a corticosteroid numbing the brain stem. When a celebrated athlete died in a car crash near Leeds on the A1 in Britain, television networks went into mourning, and packs of sycophantic bench-warming sportscasters testified how much the man's death affected them. "What did his death mean to you?" I asked Josh. "His death meant as much to me," Josh said, "as my death would have meant to him." A neighbor gave me a pile of *People* magazines. "Reading them," she said, "and others like *Time* and *Us Weekly* will help you forget writing." The magazines were opiates. I certainly forgot good writing, but their packaged stories about almost-people made me melancholy. In the early nineteenth century sensitive natures reveled in melancholia. But today at the first sign of a blue mood highly educated imbeciles recommend pharmaceuticals. It's enough to make a rational person long for the eighteenth century and healthy angry times of spleen.

Although my notebooks were locked in a drawer, I did not stop thinking about writing. I noticed little things, for example, Douglas Jerrold's remark that compared to London the country seemed "the world without its clothes on" or an article entitled "The Serpent in the Classroom" written by the parent of a little girl about to enter kindergarten. Because they appeared insignificant, I turned them about as if I were composing. I put them into declarative and interrogative sentences, recognizing that in everyday life the little are often big. One afternoon I remained in the car outside Walmart while Vicki went inside to purchase a wall clock for the kitchen. While I waited, a clerk pushed a train of thirty-two shopping baskets across the lot, and a flock of at least sixty gulls swirled around the car and tumbled onto the asphalt as if it were black sand. "Not exciting, but in any case," I preached to Vicki that evening at dinner, "such things are the threads of our moments and the fabrics of our years." "What! Is this a prelude to saying you're going to quote the letter you received last week in which your lapsed friend Wingg with two g's called Schools of Theology, Schools of Superstition?" Vicki said, picking up a falafel sandwich, the $3.99 Wednesday special from Gansett Wraps in downtown Storrs. "Certainly not," I said. "Well," she said, "what about Myrtle Reed's statement that "in order to be happy, a woman needs only a good digestion, a satisfactory complexion, and a lover. The first requirement being met; the second is not difficult to obtain, and the third follows as a matter of course." "Never.

My days are calm, and I'm too old to delight in waking Harpies," I said. "Why not?" Vicki said, "there was a time when the possibility of uncertain consequences appealed to you." She then reached into the bowl of fruit on the kitchen table and pulled out a notecard. On it I'd copied a sentence from an adventure novel I'd long forgotten. "Impermanence is the very essence of joy—the drop of bitterness that enables one to perceive the sweet."

"Have you noticed," I continued, quickly changing the subject, "that Robocall Rachel has metamorphosized into Robocall Jake without the benefit of surgery?" "You don't say," Vicki replied then bit into her sandwich. Vicki resembles my readers, attentive but not necessarily receptive. The ways of enduring wives with ancient husbands are gentler than those of rosy-cheeked milkmaids with lithe youths. Rarely, however, do wives shilly-shally about loosely on pages decorated with daisies and cowslips, nouns and verbs. Vicki doesn't like her meals seasoned with the mundane, so I did not mention the other things I'd been mulling, for instance, an up-to-date marriage ceremony based on economic reality rather than vaporous emotion. Medical insurance glues people together more firmly than love. "With this all-inclusive low annual premium policy, I thee wed," the wage earner declares. "Those whom insurance has joined together let no job change put asunder," the ministering agent responds.

Neither did I tell her that earlier in the week I dreamed that I spent two weekends going to tag sales searching for a walker. However the next morning while waiting for a lap lane in the community center swimming pool, I mentioned the dream to Jean. "There is a medical warehouse in East Hartford that sells secondhand wheelchairs, hospital beds, shower stools, and portable adult potties. I am sure you can find a sturdy walker there. Come spring I am going to purchase a walker myself. I want one that has a seat that folds down from the side, so I can sit when I become tired. Don't waste any more time thinking about exploring yard sales. Just go to East Hartford."

The previous week I read that there were "roughly 2000 species of fireflies." I did not mention the fact either because fireflies have vanished from our neighborhood. The disappearance of insects diminishes living and untunes the music of our days and nights. The losses sadden Vicki, and even though they are obvious I avoid calling attention to them. Vicki puts twigs into the dog bowls on the front and back stoops. The twigs are life-saving sticks and extend from the bottom of the bowls to the side of the house. Any insect that falls into the water at night can clamber onto a twig and haul itself out of water to safety. So far we know of only one creature who used "the ladder to safety," a seven-spotted lady bug which Vicki found at the top of the stick drying in the sun. The small number of creatures does not surprise us. In the dark moths no longer cling to the screen door or dance around the house lights. Not once during the three years we have owned our car have Vicki or I washed a bug off the wind shield. When I was a boy, in the summer Daddy drove Mommy and me from Nashville to Richmond to visit my grandparents. Most roads were two lane, and because the trip took fifteen hours, we often traveled at night. At least twice every trip Daddy pulled off the road in order to clean bugs off the wind shield.

The radii forming the web of life in our parochial world are broken. Rarely do I see many creatures that were once familiar, not just insects but also varieties of seabirds and frogs, warblers and salamanders. Several times I asked the oldest trees on the campus what could be done to repair the web. Alas, I could not understand their replies, a fact that made me realize I had been educated wrongly. I did not know the languages of trees or those of hillsides and deserts, and maybe of the human heart. The more I was schooled the more I thought I knew but the less able I was to parse the land on which I walked. Last year a publisher asked me to write a blurb for a composition handbook. I declined. One of the book's first chapters stressed the importance of "The Topic Sentence," not a subject of concern to people who frequent "genteel circles." Topic sentences are similar to jail sentences. They cage thought and imprison life. Outside the confines of a cell, ideas roam and meander naturally. Margins, lines, and paragraphs are grammatical insecticides. They are devices which limit, convenient perhaps but always distorting. Real thinking shuns neurotoxins and breaks the confinement of man-made bars. Topics jump erratically. They ignore periods and bound from one subject to another. They change as the eye moves during a picnic—there wild strawberries, here a white corporal dragonfly, overhead crows calling raucously, everywhere sentences and thoughts spinning, endings beginning and beginnings ending, and lives themselves momentarily this and that or more likely something else. Topic sentences impose structures that are illusions. Disorder or at least structures that people cannot perceive or understand make confinement appealing—all sorts of confinement: social, domestic, literary. Acknowledging and living amid dizzying incoherence makes people fabricate illusions seemingly stable with well-soldered meanings and truths. The danger or perhaps inconvenience comes when one group or person tries to force its illusion upon another group.

Telling this to Vicki would have been too much for her to swallow while eating a falafel sandwich. Although I choked occasionally when pondering topic sentences, eating was simple for me. I could not taste the falafel. Six months ago the coronavirus knocked out my senses of taste and smell. Gradually the senses have begun to creep back neuron by neuron. However the flavors of most foods and the fragrances of some flowers are different from what they were before the pandemic. I considered but decided against writing about the idiosyncrasies of my sensatory problems. Boring readers is salutary. When managed skillfully, boredom relaxes and at its best is a balm enabling sleep. In contrast descriptions of the malfunctions of gustatory processes not only can startle but they can also be in such poor taste they produce indigestion.

At another time when Vicki has irritated me to the point of biliousness, I'll describe the state of my senses in satisfactory detail. Vicki already knows I cannot taste peanut butter, blueberries, any cheese, and most breakfast cereals. I recognize the textures of All-Bran, Grape-Nuts, Go, and Shredded Wheat. Bananas are mushy as lipomas, and some mornings breakfast nauseates me almost as much as the news. "Ipecac for the mind," Josh calls it. Tart apples are bland but make passable snacks if they are crisp. On the sly I feed the Triscuits Vicki doles out to me to the dogs. Last Sunday for breakfast I had a brioche stuffed with bacon, cheddar cheese, and an egg. Accompanying it was a mound of chopped potatoes fresh from the garden and cooked with onions. I might as well have eaten a lump of sourdough bread with all the sour squeezed out. In hopes of "awakening the sleeping flavor," Vicki doused the brioche with chipotle sauce. For all the good it did she might as well have sloshed dishwater on the bread. Before the virus waylaid me, peppery dishes burned my mouth and throat. Now I don't notice hot seasoning, and curries that once made my hair burst into flame are as mild and as appealing as Vaseline.

I am also practically a teetotaler. Two sips of wine and my head aches as if the sides were being forced together in a bench clamp. After half a bottle of beer at dinner I'm looped, and I dump the other half down the kitchen sink. My mind tells me I love chocolate, and last week I ate a bowl of chocolate ice cream because no matter the state of my sense of taste I knew the cream had to be good. In truth it smacked of dung, not that I have dined on dung often, except, of course, the metaphoric variety. Meals are curiosities. I think I taste grits, but I am probably just savoring the memory of the country breakfasts of my childhood. Last week Vicki and I ate a shrimp pizza. The shrimp were lively and flavorful, but they were lodged atop a reef of dead creatures: crust, cheese, tomato sauce, and capers. Insofar as smell is concerned, the virus did not affect my enjoyment of most flowering trees and shrubs: lilac, autumn olive, magnolia, yellowwood, and oriental bittersweet, the exception being mock orange. Vicki said the raised lip at the opening to the fox den in the back yard reeked of urine. I didn't smell anything even though I bent so low sniffing I almost tumbled headfirst into the entrance. In fact, I cannot smell the droppings of any animal. This is a nuisance because when I shovel dog ends from the yard, I occasionally step in "something." In the past the fragrance was a fail-safe enabling me to discover such matter on the bottom of my shoes before I returned to the house—not now.

As I sat looking out the study window, young chipmunks racing carelessly through the grass and my mind a blank page, I wondered what I could and, maybe, ought to write. Should I unretire and start another book? The obvious subject was Sammy, Vicki's and my grandchild. We were eager as teenagers to know more about his life. For us his small doings were rich with the stuff of conversation. Like mathematicians we marveled at the statistics measuring Sammy's growth. At six months "he remains long," Edward wrote, in the 95th percentile of babies his age. He was lighter, however, than "his peers" in the lower 23rd percentile, and his head was smaller, in the 40th percentile. For others what were sterile matters of the measuring tape were for us matters of the heart. I didn't think I could translate such numbers into emotions. Moreover, I've long resisted page revelations and confidences. "Snuggling close to readers then exposing one's emotions in order to cause vicarious reactions," a younger "me" wrote thirty books ago, "differed only from picking pockets in that it was more calculated." The writer of that sentence is now another person, at least at times.

As a sharp-shinned hawk landed in a hickory and began to study the ground, I decided to leave writing about "our little boy" to Edward and Erica, and to Vicki, all of whom had already written nice things. In a recent email Vicki told Erica that she wished that the Greenville Pickerings would move to Storrs. "I really enjoy," she wrote, "seeing the idyllic atmosphere of your little household depicted in the Sammy Album photos. Summertime, a garden of sun and shade and

26

flowers of all kinds, and insects and birds. Quiet, lazy time on a blanket or in the rocking chair in the shade of the front verandah with greenery and plants all around. You have built, in so many respects, a perfect little existence in Greenville. It would be hard or impossible to duplicate the comfort of your home and its beautiful grounds that you have cultivated with so much love, hard to duplicate all the activities and attractions of downtown Greenville within walking distance. But I know that you are uncomfortable with the local political climate and future educational possibilities for Sammy. And I realize you always keep the idea of moving in the back of your heads. Know that you will always be welcomed and wanted here."

The morning after writing Erica, Vicki came downstairs at 9:15. She had not slept well. A dream exhausted her. She was unable to talk, she explained, because she had lost her breath fighting ropes of "dark poisonous snakes." Later she said the biggest snake was still alive and hiding behind the refrigerator. "He's too frightened to show his head and bother us," she added reassuringly. "He'll never be seen again. His days of hissing are over. Some silent moment when we are not in the house, he'll crawl outside, slither down a hole, and vanish into a safe human-less netherworld." The dream was a stunning contrast to Vicki's sentimental email, but then people are bundles of moods and incongruities.

Improper English and trite expressions make me erupt in expletives. On Saturday a eulogist used *passed* to refer to a dead acquaintance. I almost interrupted the man saying that corpses lose the ability to pass. "The dead have experienced their last breakdowns. Their gas lines have burst like aneurisms. Their wheels have run off their ligaments, and they are permanently and irreparably on the shoulder of life, memories of them fast oxidizing." Time has shaved so much off the capacities and interests of people my age that our lives and conversation are similar. When the elderly meet, they inevitably discuss their health using the same words, not just the names of diseases that plague them but the same phrases. I cannot bear to hear the expression "organ recital" again. I don't sputter cacophonously, but I quickly absent myself from broken and out of key pipes. "On some happy day I'm going away," as the gospel song puts it. At the moment I'm still on my legs, but so many friends have reached their eleventh hour that sometimes I think myself a conductor standing on the platform beside the sleeper attached to The Midnight Special crying "All Aboard."

"To Our Guests," reads a sign at the door of Price Chopper. "As we all move forward into a new and better normal, we will continue to make the well-being of our guests and teammates our top priority." "Customers and employees!" I said to Vicki. "This notice smacks of the credentialism that pervades society—university teachers bookending their names with 'Dr.' and 'Ph.D.,' their salutations followed by a donkey's tail of parochial posts and committee assignments similar to things kids who were almost secretary-treasurers of their high school senior classes once listed under their names in yearbooks." "Didn't you have the longest list in your class at MBA?" Vicki asked. "Yes," I answered but that was in 1959, and in 1930 when mother graduated from St. Catherine's, the space below her name was blank." The use of inflated, inexact language is at its most harmless a sign of pulpy thought. At the worst, it reveals slipperiness of character, a person who, if not consciously malicious, thinks so sloppily that whatever he says is untrustworthy and rarely matters.

Vicki thinks drawing strong conclusions from grammatical errors, trite sayings, and pretentious language is wrong. She is right. If topic sentences resemble jail sentences, then proper English and elegant language are the tops and bottoms of jail uniforms. They restrict and distort, and once a person throws them off, he may range creatively, idiosyncratically, and perhaps more thoughtfully, albeit nakedly. No person lives what he writes. How can I urge people to escape topic sentences while simultaneously criticizing them for eschewing "correct" English and stripping off the prison garb of language? The answer is "I can." To be alive is to be inconsistent. Only the actions of a person who has "passed" are consistent. However, the things he did while living are likely to be misinterpreted and wrung out of shape and into inconsistency by family and if he was prominent by strangers.

"There are no easy answers," as Vicki's father said when asked a thorny question, his reply both a truth and an evasion. Life is more serene if a person neither asks nor answers questions. The truly wise never hesitate to say, "I do not know." Inconsistency tormented the preacher Frederick Robertson, the fact that while his tastes were with the aristocracy, his principles were with the mob. Quite so and quite normal. Stock car racing, "The Batchelor," and cannibalistic holidays smoky with grilled meats may be so removed from a person's cultural caste that the people who enjoy such things nauseate him. Yet, withal he may advocate, if not believe in, a horn of equalities: opportunity, education, income, indeed of souls. He may quote the Beatitudes blessing people whom he studiously avoids and with whom he never associates, in linguistic terms people from "the bottom rail" who say, "between you and they." Abiding with the self is easier if one erases conundrums from the mind. They muddy lives and prose. Purging them transforms nervous, erratic breathing into soothing sleep. Better it is to submerge thought in blissful indefiniteness and to cap wells of criticism with partially true declarative statements, two favorites of mine that I occasionally believe, the first, Edwin Whipple's "What we call law and order are other names for injustice and oppression," the second, "only fools break eggs in the middle."

When an agitated "seeker" pesters me, I often suggest that he spend the rest of the day, indeed week, meditating on the dangers of idleness. That usually elicits the monosyllabic, conversation-ending response "what?" When an acquaintance retired into "meaningless days" bleats "Why am I living?" I imagine replying like an undertaker in training and saying, "you just are and will continue to do so until you stop." However, a grain of slippery verbal craft prevents dyspepsia and ends the conversation quicker and more satisfactorily than a pound of truth. Usually, I slip the moment and change the subject by exhuming a tale so long buried that only a button from its waistcoat remains. "Did you hear about the ancient moneybags who handed a bottle of wine to his young doxy commending it for its age?" I recently asked a depressed neighbor. "'Humph, all I can say,' the gal remarked as she looked at the bottle, 'is that it's very small for its age.'" Once I quoted Arthur Helps's remark, "It would be comparatively much less difficult to invent a plausible account of the meaning and purpose of this world if it were only inhabited by human beings. But the existence of animals complicates the question hugely." "Do mean dogs?" the woman to whom I was speaking said. "My Gallic 'boule dogue' Hunegund has a saint's name, but she isn't a Christian, and neither is Sadie's [her daughter] hamster."

While holidaying from writing, I read the obituaries of acquaintances. I did so to pass time. Additionally unearthing the makings of lively pages would be useful if I recanted, mounted a literary nag, and again wielded my pencil. "You won't last long in the lists if your sentences canter as awkwardly as that," Vicki commented. Romping boys are not perceptive, and many people with whom I spent little time grew into individuals I wish I'd known. Things that separated people and created obstacles that appeared so insurmountable that one did not question them now seemed preposterous. The most harmful and the most absurd was race. How I wondered could a society ever believe race mattered? I don't feel guilty because during the time I was a child my world taught otherwise. All societies are rag bags. In some ways and places, race mattered; in others it didn't, schooling being an example of the first, affection for individuals an example of the second. Religions with their doctrinaire superstitions are another matter. Last week while Josh and I sat outside a café sipping coffee, a man strode by wearing a T-shirt on the back of which was printed, "I Am A Child of GOD." "Rubbish," Josh exclaimed, "I know my three children well, and that halfwit is not one of them. How blasphemously presumptuous!" As the gospel song should have put it, "Give me that old time Episcopalian for whom a country club and a charming social mate are a damn sight good enough."

Complicating reading obituaries and recalling lost years were that the recollections of octogenarians are shaky. My memory is better than that most of the "old-tarded." Rarely, however, do I say "remember when" because the person I'm addressing likely won't remember. Also, I have lost track of most old friends. The bed boards beneath which a few rest their heads have become body snatcher's stones. Others have lost me and themselves in dementia. In any case all are sleepy figures in my remembered life, and since I am something of a Sadducee, I don't expect them to spring from the grave tossing batons into the air and like an alarm clock singing, "My, oh, my, what a wonderful day." My real life is a bustling place crowded with people most of whom I make up. Their doings interest and involve me. Although others may find them tedious, they don't bore me unless I want them to do so which, of course, amuses me. I try to control them, but sometimes I fail.

The nightcrawlers who appear in dreams are the most difficult to manage. One day two weeks ago I woke Vicki before dawn to describe "Johnny Milano, a tough cookie with a dark streak in his character." He didn't interest Vicki. "Even sleep doesn't impose a moratorium on your punning, and most are terrible," she said. "Despite appearing a little too smooth—zoot-suitish—he can be sweet," I replied then got out of bed. I left the bedroom, but Johnny lingered. He was one of my from the wrong side of the sheet offspring. The next night he fulminated against the reflexive use of pat phrases that appear to convey concern and emotion but which are empty. "Corrupting," Johnny said, "substituting words for deeds." The catalyst for Johnny's remark was an obituary I received in the mail that afternoon. It described the life of a man I knew slightly and had been sent to me by a distant acquaintance. At the bottom of the obituary my correspondent wrote, "I have said a prayer for him and prayer is all." "And less costly than flowers," Johnny said, "and one of those 'easier said than done's.'"

The hearts of my imaginary companions skip in startling arrythmias. After graduating from Sewanee, my classmate A. Hotep Tillis, IV did not become a banker or a lawyer as his family expected. Instead, he attended the Owen School of Management at Vanderbilt. After graduating he founded the Giza Company and became a formaldehyde salesman. The company manufactured three gradations of formaldehyde: the Menkaure, short-lasting, but a satisfactory sealant protecting against flesh flies and coffin beetles and thus suitable for quick pottings, the Khafre, guaranteed to prevent cadaveric spasms and priced to meet the needs and tastes of most weepers, and finally the Cheops, the super glue of binders, warrantied to hold beloved corpses together indefinitely, making them suitable for glass coffins and living room displays. This spring for the twenty-second year running at the annual meeting of the Southern Formaldehyde Association (SFASS) held in Pascagoula, Mississippi, Hotep was selected as Formaldehyde Salesman of the Year. Because of the virus, he recounted, sales were so good that he bought two retirement getaways, one on Sanibel Island, the other a small flat in Montmartre, these in addition to houses he owned on Martha's Vineyard and in Belle Meade, Tennessee. As a schoolboy, Hotep had a poetic bent, and I was surprised he didn't pursue a Ph.D. in English and teach at a small college. Still, he decorated the labels on his formaldehyde containers with lyrics, the most famous being, "When the trumpets call from on high, / From the grave I will rise to the sky, / Shouting 'Oh, My Lord, I am ready to serve,' / My body saccharine-sweet, incorruptible, and preserved."

Soon I will probably begin writing again although I will avoid mortality bills. Life is rich, and writing forces me to notice and appreciate, to record and make new memories at a time when most good memories have become brittle and crazed. On Tuesday I had my yearly Wellness Physical. How well can an eighty-year-old be unless he is a Marvel Superhero? Ailments are us. Ken did the parsing. He has been my doctor and the doctor of my family for over forty years. He is a friend, and his knowledge of me and mine of him go deeper than stethoscope and tongue depressor. Seeing him makes me think myself a member of a community, something difficult in a university town in which most people are students and temporary residents. Many faculty live in distant towns and come and go without putting down roots. For their part administrators are epiphytes. After their roots absorb enough money from the air they disappear. For decades Ken has studied ticks and tick-borne diseases. He knows that arachnids, indeed most small creepers and crawlers, intrigue me, and after the examination he led me into his office. On a table sat a microscope and two score petri dishes containing ticks. He showed me one. In the dish was a tick he'd removed from a woman's back. The tick was female and a few days after being extracted gave birth. The eggs clustered around their mother's body, under the microscope looking like caviar, golden and American, trout eggs, not sturgeon, black and Russian like Beluga. What a sight, one that whetted my appetite for seeing!

Although I am almost anonymous, people are

aware of the delight I take in nature. "You are no Thoreau," a man told me in Dog Lane Café three years ago, "but your writing is all right, and that's good enough for people hereabouts." "There is a day when the road neither comes nor goes, and the way is not a way but a place," Wendel Berry wrote—yes, a place with its creatures and people. Last month the man sent me an account of finding a newly hatched painted turtle on his lawn. The turtle was the size of a quarter and its tail as long as the nail on the man's little finger. The turtle was crawling toward the deck under which a raccoon sometimes "hung out," so the man picked it up and put it in a Pyrex dish with a little water, broccoli florets, two raisins, and a climbing rock. The turtle was soon atop the rock and ready to move on. The man debated where to free the turtle. He ruled out a patch of tiger lilies because he'd seen garter snakes there. Eventually he placed the turtle in the shade under a clematis vine. There the soil was soft and rich with earthworms. The turtle was a wanderer, though, and soon it set off across the lawn toward some rocks and a lodging of his choice. "Fare forward, wee painted figure, and grow," the man said as he watched the turtle disappear.

My friend Phil sent an account of an American success story. Phil's brother Kerry lived in Missouri. Before he was diagnosed with Alzheimer's, Kerry gave his therapist a Cadillac and "much, much money" after which she decamped. "The old tale describing the generosity of the impaired," Phil wrote. "Because I'm wheelchair and house bound, I lack the energy to deal with the matter. 'Good luck to the therapist' is about all I can say. Some people rob folks our age with a pen, some with a thermometer, others with a telephone call." Phil said he should have acted a year

35

ago immediately after Kerry asked what summer the two of them worked as councilors in an Arab Day Camp for children "located on an old paddle wheeler moored to a bank on the Missouri River." He also wanted to know the identity of the tiny man tied to him by a "tiny rope" and who accompanied him everywhere he went. "Kerry's decline is upsetting," Phil concluded. "But I made a warehouse of dough and can pay to keep him in a good nursing home. You know the old statement, 'Fat sorrow is better than lean sorrow.'"

Does everyone my age become a funeral registry? Two days after hearing from Phil, I received a letter from Reg, a college classmate. For the aged, Time is simultaneously long and short, a day seeming years, and years, a day. Forty-five years ago, I wrote Reg. He did not answer. Now unexpectedly, he sent a full account of his life and the lives of his family. "Rays from the Mystical Sun cured me," Reg's terminally ill brother Clyde told him. "The cure was short-lived. Clyde died thirty-six hours later," Reg recounted. "His spiritual advisor urged me to cremate Clyde and sprinkle his ashes in the Ganges. The virus made travel impossible, so I dumped Clyde in the Mississippi River near the ruins of Fort Pickering." Reg and Clyde came from a wealthy Southern family that had bred themselves into oddity. Although their mother graduated from Sweetbriar, country nostrums filled her medicine cabinet. When the family members had upset stomachs, she drenched them with stinging nettle tea. During their elementary school years whenever the boys came down with sore throats, she made them hold a snake doctor [Southern name for dragonfly] under their tongues for half an hour. She kept a ready supply of insects on hand. After catching them she froze them and stored the bodies in a jar in the freezer. "When our friends were getting shots and swallowing pills, mother scheduled appointments with snake doctors. I liked it," Reg said. "It made us different."

Letters bring miscellanies of things to mind. Reg believed the reference to Fort Pickering would appeal to me. It didn't. Instead I thought about my common-sensical life devoid of seances, meditation, the musky aroma of ectoplasm, holy rivers, and mind-altering chemicals. I never put a snake doctor in my mouth; I only caught them and marveled at their beauty. No god or any of his winged or tusked minions has addressed me from above, and no corpse has spoken to me from below. I've never danced with a fairy, run from a warlock or been chauffeured about in a Rolls-Royce. I jogged but didn't practice Yoga. As a child I couldn't stand on my head or do a somersault. The one time I tried a hoola-hoop, it fell to my ankles and tripped me. I'm a plodder and an anecdote-monger. No one brags that he has met me. In all things I am a minor league guy. That's where the fun is, not in the majors. Because I am a journeyman and have never hit a homerun, no one goes to the trouble of throwing a "high hard one" at my head.

Mine has been a life of walks and strolls and restful, splinter-less times on the bench. As a result, I have been as happy as a tumble bug in a dairy. "Or a pecker gnat on a foreskin," Vicki said. Rarely, however, does such a quiet life, or better perhaps the absence of life, attract readers. Consequently, to add a little intoxicating hop to my pages, I occasionally purloin ideas. "You are not a plagiarist," my friend Josh assures me. "Your ideas are as old as the itch and appeared in books before the invention of the printing press. In that editorial you wrote last week didn't you borrow a couple of lines from Laney Linden's bestseller *Hug Your Own Heart*? 'Don't ruin today worrying about tomorrow. You won't be alone in the afterlife. Decent people have as many friends in Hell as they do in Heaven.' Furthermore, I know you aren't the first person to write that when men are twenty, they love woman, 'at thirty, a woman, and at forty, women.'" Josh was right, but I did not tell him so. Reformation by confession rarely endures the wound it inflicts upon conceit.

I answered Reg. I said I was sorry about Clyde. After packaged responses about the gay "old days" and how splendid it was to renew our acquaintance, I mentioned that recently I'd sprained ligaments in my right knee. "A nuisance I'm treating with a course of balneotherapy." That's an uptown way of saying I was soaking my knee, balneotherapy likely familiar to someone whose brother waffled on endlessly about the numinous and the materialization of the dematerialized. Phishing among the old consists of writing letters in hopes of landing responses. If an addressee takes the bait and replies, then the angler responds with another letter. In hopes of throwing the hook before Reg began an extended correspondence, I told him I was reading *Billy Whiskers*. "More instructive than Proverbs," I wrote, "the ideal book for Christian Conversion Societies to distribute to misbehaving Baptists and Mohammedans. Teenagers tottering on the precipice of puberty will especially benefit from the description of Billy's affection for his wife Nanny." Reg did not write again.

On the less rueful side of life, Charles sent me a copy of William Glackens's painting "The Soda Fountain" owned by the Museum of Fine Arts in

Philadelphia and painted in 1935, six years before I was born. The painting is visual twaddle, its content nostalgic and soothing, not whipping thought into a headache. It's the sort of painting that makes aged viewers recall sweet moments in the past: Moon's drugstore next to the Belle Meade Theater in Nashville where Betty Lou made milkshakes on Saturday afternoon before and after movies seventy years ago or Candyland where I walked down West End from the Sulgrave Apartments with Daddy and where Mr. Pappas made us double chocolate sodas. In that hollow phrase "the great scope of things," such memories are insignificant. But in an actual life led by an individual, they matter immensely, especially if one moved away from the wellspring of recollection before its freshness dissipated. They are not things which can be stitched into importance. They are soda days sugary with ice cream and light with sparkling water. They are things which make lives livable and satisfying.

On the canvas, two girls sit at a counter in a drugstore, the soda fountain visible across the counter. The back of the girl on the left faces the viewer. She wears a light-red dress, a silk scarf, a straw hat with a ribbon of flowers circling the crown, and like her companion kid gloves. She is waiting for her soda, and her left arm is bent and resting on her hip. The other girl faces the viewer. On her head is a jaunty sailor cap, and she wears a yellow dress. She slumps against the counter and having finished her soda uses her right hand to wipe her lips with a silk handkerchief. Her left hand presses a summer purse against her middrift. Dressed in a white uniform and standing on a slightly raised platform, the soda jerk is pulling a lever and soda water is streaming into a glass below the level of the counter. On the counter are sundry things, among others, a stainless-steel milk shake cup filled with straws, a shorter cup holding spoons, two bottles looking like quarts of Coca-Cola and then on a side shelf a pineapple resting on a foundation of lemons and apples.

In the late 1940s and early 1950s, the "Happiness Club" met at Belle Meade Theater on Saturday afternoon. Admission cost sixteen cents, and a talent show took place before the movie was shown. The performers were usually our elementary school peers although I remember a young Pat Boone's appearing once. The movies themselves featured cowboys or cartoon animals. At the end of the talent show, children in the audience sang, "Happy days are here again! / The skies above are clear again. / Let us sing a song of cheer again. / Happy days are here again!" After the movie, we drank milkshakes until our parents fetched us. Alas, our Saturday-afternoon friend The Singing Cowboy Gene Autry is no longer home on the screen. He is a permanent resident of a distant Red River Valley and won't be back in the saddle again.

For her part Betty Lou graduated from the soda fountain. She got a Ph.D. in English from the University of California at Irvine. Afterward she taught Shakespeare at a college outside Chicago for three decades. She was a textual scholar specializing in emending corrupted manuscripts. Her best-known improvement focused on the three Witches or Weird Sisters in *Macbeth*. They appeared in the first scene of the play amid a symphony of thunder and lightning, that is, near dinner time, saying, "Fair is foul, and foul is fair." Betty Lou believed the line made no sense. In the fourth act the Sisters reappeared traipsing around a cauldron, in Irma Rombauer's terms, a deep-dish cooking pot. Into the pot they threw a spice cabinet of seasonings: the toe of a frog, a newt's eye, a lizard's leg, baboon blood, a Turk's nose, and a Tartar's lips, among other delicacies. The gals were, of course, concocting a seventeenth century version of Brunswick stew. Because chickens had long been the cackling familiars of witches and sorcerers, Professor Elizabeth Louise wrote, "it is obvious chickens constituted the dish's main ingredient. Consequently, to anyone aware of culinary matters, the line in act one must read, "Fare is fowl, and fowl is fare."

As for me, my days are soda-less and don't effervesce as they once did. I am the silver-headed daddy of three grown children. I am following the footsteps of the Singing Cowboy. I'm headed for the last roundup and no longer canter to the tune of jingle, jangle, jingle. In Vicki's and my kitchen half hidden by the refrigerator and leaning against a rack of cabinets is my Father's Day present, a pair of ski poles. "To make walking easier and safer," Vicki said. After Vicki showed them to me, I said, "You always have my best interests at heart. Thank you." What I thought was, "Nuts." On the counter in front of me was a platter of apples, Macouns, crisp and juicy. "Will you hand me one?" Vicki asked. "Sure," I said. For a moment I considered taking a bite out of it first. Old-school gentlemen always sample apples before handing them to women. They do so to excise unaesthetic bruises and to insure that the fruits are not wormy.

# End of the Roads

The end of my road is a dead end, and my days have narrowed so much that turning around is impossible. In December Vicki's and my only grandson Little Sammy Pickering was born in Greenville, South Carolina. We agreed that as soon as feasible, we'd drive to Greenville and meet him, well, hug and kiss him. Because of snow, the virus, our ailments, and a rolodex of springtime doctors' appointments, we didn't leave Connecticut until the last day of June. I insisted on driving—a decision influenced by fumes from past trips, not a deadly gas but one that dulls the intellect. I never liked driving, but through the years I made rotaries of trips: back and forth from Nashville to Portland, Maine, from Connecticut to Houston and back, a roundabout from Storrs to Eureka Springs Arkansas, 2880 miles, New Jersey to West Texas, innumerable treks from Tennessee to Richmond, most on dizzying two lane roads, and then stutterings up and down the coast of Western Australia driving a station wagon rollicking with children.

"The idea of travelling has long seduced you," Vicki said. "Because you have aged, now you only book cruises, but in greener times, you sailed on passenger liners and rode the rails. Walking railway tracks when you were a boy endowed trains with an irresistible magic." Vicki was right. Distant whistles drew me to track beds. The sight of sleepers awakened my imagination, and the names on boxcars were free verse luring me beyond the moment: the Atchison, Topeka, and the Santa Fe, and the N.C. and St. L., this last the old Nashville, Chattanooga, and Saint Louis. The trains I rode were various, but even the locals were alluring. From the hindsight of days tacked together by pills, some of the trips seem exotic: in the mid-1960s riding a student train from London to Vienna then on to Budapest and Bucharest, returning by way of Sofia and Belgrade, the Red Arrow Express from Leningrad to Moscow knifing through the night in a snowstorm, and then journeys across Australia on the Indian Pacific from Perth to Sydney then back to Perth.

As our children grew, place and responsibility, maybe the belief I needed to save money for schools, changed the nature of travelling. Language tames the unruly and conventionalizes. For fifty years I reviewed travel books and wandered the world almost without leaving my desk. The book travels were satisfactory. Nevertheless, like a bacteria, the hankering for actual travel lingered in my liver. Otherwise, I wouldn't have insisted that Vicki and I not fly to Greenville but drive, 932 miles down and 926 back. Age makes a person less capable but not always more rational. The trip was worse than the bad behavior of the famous little girl who had a curl in the middle of her forehead. It was horrid. We set out at 9:11 in the morning on June 30, having taken the dogs to the kennel and filled the car with gas the previous day. Aging bodies make demands, and during the trip we paused at practically every rest stop. Our first pause was on the shoulder of Interstate 84, ninety-seven miles from home and within speeding distance of a rest stop and its Necessary House. I obey the speed limit, however, and when nature calls the elderly, it doesn't whisper. It caterwauls. During the trip I stopped a couple of times on the shoulders of interstates. "You might have been arrested," Josh said after we returned home. "Absolutely not," I said. "People obey me, and I wouldn't have allowed it."

What did not obey was the traffic and the weather. At Wilkes-Barre Pennsylvania, we spent an hour and eleven minutes in a traffic jam. On Interstate 85, the last leg of the trip to Greeneville, we got stuck for another hour between Charlotte and Spartanburg. In Maryland and later in the mountains of southern Virginia, thunderstorms obliterated the road. In each case lanes vanished. I drove white-knuckled and followed the taillights of trucks ahead, breaking into operatic vulgarity every time their lights flickered and went out. The worst part of the trip was Route 81, the truckers' highway south from Wilkes-Barre, America's asphalt River Styx. For mile after enduring mile trucks loomed behind, in front, and beside us like schools of mythological ravenous megatheria, grills slavering and motors bilious and growling. Trucks outnumbered cars. "Females in their breeding years avoid the states of the old Confederacy and the septic legislatures intent on blighting women's lives," Vicki concluded, after studying automobiles that passed us. "The only people headed South are tax refugees, all beyond child bearing years, people interested more in golf than procreation, not one even knowing the meaning of enceinte." "How do our Greenville Pickerings fit that pattern? I asked. "They don't," Vicki said; "perhaps if we promise to pay their state and property taxes they'll move to Connecticut."

The temperature was in the 90s, and a gray cloud of exhaust fumes hung over the highway polluting the air and soiling conversation. The fields that once swept across southern Pennsylvania and the northern Shenandoah Valley fat with corn, black Angus, and apple trees had become distribution centers--huge white buildings that smothered the land, hives with tractor trailers swarming in and out of cells like drones—all dead to the eye and deadening the heart. "Erysipelas of a society in which money constitutes the only beauty," Josh said later. Interstate cuisine causes indigestion, and by the end of our four days coming and going, meals consisted of McDoubles and coffee. We spent the first night in Harrisonburg. We were so tired that when we left the Interstate motel signs vanished like mirages, and the only motel we found was an Econolodge. The next morning we drove to a McDonald's for breakfast. The employees were not native English speakers, and no one understood my Southern accent. On the return trip we stayed at a Travelodge in Winchester. Fenil the night clerk was from Guarat. On the counter stood a sign saying the charge for having a pet in one's room was ten dollars. Fenil said the oddest pet he'd admitted to the motel was a turkey. Sitting in the lobby were two women. One wore a shirt that read, "A Mole Doesn't Need A Flashlight," the other, "Rats Run Down Sewers." The motel was near a Cracker Barrel, a happy change from McDonald's. When his mother became ill, Malek our waiter left college to nurse her and to earn money for medicines. "I want to return," he said. "There's so much I want to do in life." In another restaurant L.J. told me his initials stood for Lonnie Junior and that both his father and brother were named Lonnie, the father with no middle name, the brother Lonnie II.

Pickerings are small town people. Grandfather Pickering sold insurance and, Father said, knew everyone in Smith County. From college I carried away tales not ideas. Personalities and the storied world of the classroom clung to me long after thoughts shredded into compost. Later the classes I taught were anecdotal, the books and students themselves anthologies, their pages bound together by the mucilage of living, the accounts particular and never abstract no matter how strangely imagined or experienced. I have written much about travel and home. Wherever the location, I seem to be on a street corner, gesturing and chatting with a stranger. I notice important events, but none appear on my pages. On the fourth of July, Vicki and I watched fireworks standing amid two trucks of firemen on hand to douse unexpected fires. One man had been a fireman for 33 years. He planned to retire in the next two years. Many firemen, he said, did not live long. Fire-retardant chemicals and the carelessness with which they were used before people learned they were carcinogenic caused cancer. Firemen often had side businesses, the man said. Two of his friends turned old fire hoses into hats. "I raise and sell boxer dogs. I have only one female and don't have a puppy farm. At the moment, I am waiting for a male to clear quarantine and arrive from Spain." He said he researched his animals' bloodlines. Raising the boxers took much care, but as a result, his dogs were in demand, the sales enabling him to buy farmland, put his two sons through college, and recently to pay for his daughter's wedding. "The most money I ever made in a year was $32,000. I always make more than $13,000." The conversation made me question what I knew and wonder if I had really lived. Was "buried in a book" not metaphoric but an accurate description of a teacher's life. Unlike my muddiness, Vicki's reaction was clear. "People should not breed dogs. Bronson McFaddle should be ashamed. If a person wants a pet, he can get one at an animal shelter." Vicki doesn't talk to strangers. Instead she pins names on them, recently, Kaillyn Overburk, Molar Farnsby, Bronson's married sister Lanie Lowden, and Harriet Trillingsworth, an art dealer who for the first thirty years of her life was Festine Figer.

Vicki and I spent eleven nights at Homewood Suites by Hilton on South Main Street. In motels Vicki doesn't let suitcases touch the floor in order to prevent crawlies from burrowing into our clothes. Homewood Suites was new and sparkling. Its employees were scrubbed and gracious, and the only bacterial beings in our room were us. Our suite consisted of a sitting room, a bedroom, a bath, and a kitchen. The rooms were so big that we lost track of where we put things. In each of the two main rooms, a large television hung on the wall, and broad windows, big enough to jump out of easily, let in sunlight. Besides the rooms the booking included underground parking and a buffet breakfast, better than Sunday brunch at a country club, the only unappetizing offering a wall television always tuned to Fox. For the accommodations we paid less than we did to board our dogs in Storrs. The hotel was on South Main, downtown's central street that crossed Reedy River and became North Main and a thorough fare of shops, cafes, and restaurants. Practically every morning after breakfast we walked three blocks and had a cappuccino and a morning bun at Old Europe. We sat outside at a table on the sidewalk and looked at people. Many people pushed baby carriages. The population of Storrs is old, and one sees more canes than carriages. Other people walked dogs. The dogs never barked or showed their teeth. Only once did we see a dog urinate. "Their owners must fill their dinner bowls with horsetails and mix oxybutynin and trospium in their Pedigree," Vicki said.

Usually, Edward and Erica and Sammy joined us. Afterward we rummaged through shops and galleries, ate in small restaurants, explored the Farmers' Market, and sauntered through Reedy Falls Park following the Swamp Rabbit Trail. The town became familiar. By the end of our stay, I recognized a score of afflicted people, among others, the man who wore a Panama hat tilted to the right side of his head and walking purposely always seemed preoccupied, the fast talker who asked questions about geography, the beggar who sat on a stairwell, held a white Styrofoam cup, and whispered "please, please," the addict with white bare gums who staggered purposely down the center of streets rapping on car windows and asking for money for food. "Pretty woman," she said to Vicki, "I'm hungry." The most poignant was a handsome young man who roamed the streets clutching a big teddy bear under his left arm. In a sense Storrs is not America, and I never see such unfortunates.

In Greenville people born in South Carolina were rarities or at least out of sight in warehouses or storerooms. Most people I met in Greenville were either tourists or "settlers" from other states. Waitresses and clerks could not understand my Southern accent, and in voices that smacked of central Europe or the far east asked where I was from, leaving Vicki to shake her head and translate my reply. African Americans were the exception. When we talked, we visited. Along Marrow Bone Creek in Lake Conestee several turtles sunned themselves on logs. I asked a likely looking countryman if he could identify the turtles. "Are they sliders or cooters or maybe Southern painted turtles?" I asked. "I can't see them very well." "I don't know," the man said. "I moved here two years ago to get away from the snow. I'm from Bangor, Maine." The only immediately identifiable South Carolinians were Edward's neighbors and the drivers of pickup trucks who cruised through downtown Greenville. The trucks were not practical farm vehicles, their sides scratched and bruised, beds earthy and broken-hinged with the lingering perfume of manure. Instead, they were statement trucks--domestic and political diminutives of tractor trailers that rumbled lawlessly through the mind. Work had not chipped their paint, and despite their muscular hoods and fenders looked as if they'd recently had facials. They were noisy and as they passed through town snarled aggressively, "thumping their chests." "Trucks that passersby cannot ignore," Vicki said, "driven, of course, by the unnoticeable, people who become invisible once they leave the cabs—nobody guys cruising the streets going nowhere."

Across South Main from Homewood Suites was Fluor Field, home of the Drive, Greenville's Class A baseball team. The Drive was an affiliate of the Boston Red Sox, and the ballpark was a replica of Fenway in Boston. I live a minor-league life punctuated by balks and singles but never a complete game or home run. Each time I was called up to the majors, I worked hard to be sent down, refusing interviews, turning down speeches, even leaving the country and going on absent reserve. I've always preferred sitting on benches and observing rather than being observed, not playing to crowds but musing to some muted pencil-tapping inner beat. In his *Characteristics* Shaftesbury said that it was the hardest thing in the world to be a good thinker without being a good self-examiner. That may be true. What is certainly true is that in the presence of a first grandchild, people's attentions are usually not on themselves. Happily, they are too besotted to indulge in abstract thought. I cannot explain the reason, but major leagues have always repulsed me. In contrast minor-leagues draw me like honey. One night the five of us watched a game between the Drive and the Aberdeen Iron Birds, an affiliate of the Baltimore Orioles based in Aberdeen, Maryland.

The game started at seven o'clock, and we sat at the end of Row K in Section 101 on the shady side of the field. Edward and Erica took turns holding Sammy who lasted until the beginning of the sixth inning. We fortified ourselves against tedium by each drinking a beer. Vicki was hungry, so at the beginning of the third inning she went to the "Fowl Pole" and bought a chicken burger. The evening was entertaining and special as it was "Bark in the Park" night and packs of dogs watched the game. Between innings they chased Frisbees, raced through plastic tunnels, leapt over low fences, competed in whipped cream eating contests, and visited with one another scampering about in high spirits. During the "Star-Spangled Banner," more dogs sang than spectators. At the gate we were given a bobble-head creation depicting Greg Burgess, the Drive's "Vice-President of Grounds and Operations." Greg was six and a half inches tall and stood on a thick slab of green turf. His hands were on his hips, elbows out, and he wore gray shorts, a short-sleeved red souvenir shirt, and a black baseball cap with the Drive's logo on the crown. Greg was bearded, and when he was picked up, his head shook like he suffered from the palsy, At his feet three boxer dogs sat on their haunches: Maggie who was twelve years old and loved drinking from the "irrigation heads," Murphy who died at two and half while playing fetch, and Muda born in August 2019, and whose name was short for Bermuda, the grass not the island. The Canine Healing Project run by the Noble Dog Hotel underwrote the souvenir. The project was "dedicated to saving at risk dogs," some going to "forever" homes, others becoming community therapy dogs. At the moment Greg and his pack are in the middle of our dining room table. Eventually they'll be kenneled in the basement, another item for our children to dispose of in a tag sale after we die.

The game was good fun. I resuscitated a couple yells from my high school baseball days, urging pitchers to put the Egyptian spin on their throws, and remarking that some pitches looked like aspirins going sideways. None of the gang joined me, but a couple of folks sitting behind us encouraged me, saying "you're telling them." Players on both teams were young. There were no former major leaguers eking out playing days, and although a couple of players were from Venezuela, most were from small towns or places unfamiliar to me, Houlka, Mississippi; Wyncote, Pennsylvania; Lithonia, Georgia; and Bridge City, Texas, for example. One hard-throwing pitcher was from Methuen, Massachusetts, and had attended the University of Connecticut. When he pitched, I howled, but he could not distinguish my Husky cry from the yowling of four-legged canines. The Drive won the game 6-5, not that it mattered as only rarely could I see the ball. It was a musical night in mood and for the ear. Spectators sang "Take Me Out to the Ballgame," "Who Let the Dogs Out," and "Sweet Caroline," all with more fervor than they sang the national anthem.

Before leaving Greenville, I returned to Fluor

Field and bought a souvenir tee-shirt. The shirt is mostly blue. On the front appear Greenville and Baseball in red. Sandwiched between them is Drive in white. To the side is the team logo, a big G, the ending a horizontal stroke sweeping across the middle finishing in what resembles the primary feathers of a bird's wing and symbolizing speed or flight. I wore it two days after I returned to Storrs. I thought it would be a conversation starter and add diversity to the haberdashery of tee-shirts saying Huskies, Red Sox, or Yankees. I was disappointed. No one, not even people who knew me remarked on the shirt. "How many people are going to comment on a shirt worn by an eighty year old stranger? You are the only person who'd do that." Vicki said. "What did you say to the woman wearing the shirt that read 'I Run Like the Winded'?" "I cannot remember," I said. "Well, I remember that every time a soul-saver said, 'Have a Blessed Day,' you replied, 'Amen. Praise King Jesus and all the Sanctified Crew.'"

Baseball may furnish words for paragraphs. But that distorts. We were in Greenville to see Little Sammy, and his presence filled our days. We roamed the woods with him and accompanied him to Goldfish Swim School. We ate meals in restaurants and at his parent's house with him. We held him and kissed him. We washed and fed him. I rolled him through town in his baby carriage and along paths in gardens and state parks. He liked rhyme and rhythm, and I recited scores of nursery rhymes that I'd forgotten. At night we talked about him, his smiles, bright joyful eyes, his playfulness, our hopes and dreams for him, these last always tempered by fears. We scrolled back through the years and tried to recall the babyhoods of Francis, Edward, and Eliza. The particulars had vanished, but we had Sammy and that was good enough. He was our fountain of youth. The pains and weariness that every day make me hanker for the grave vanished. When we left Greenville, we wept, "making driving these busy roads goddamn hard," I said to Vicki, an imprecation provoked by the realization that ahead of us far from Sammy and his parents our lives would be diminished. Are we fond silly grandparents? No, he is the absent love of old age, akin to but not the same as the lost loves of youth. When the melancholy fit falls upon us, we are too old to follow Keats's suggestion and glut our sorrow on the rainbow or morning rose. They are fine lovely things, but they are not Sammy.

Similarities between generations of family please people as they age. As the skein of a person's life unravels into a short thread, ties linking the past to the present generate a welcome continuance, one that promises to extend into and perhaps beyond the immediate future creating the illusion of immortality. Unlike the old who embrace belonging and for whom individuality has lost its allure and smacks of arid isolation and ending, the young want to be unique, self-created, or to emend the delusory words of Cassius, masters not simply of their fates but of their days. Mother's father possessed a magical green touch and was a florist and lover of trees and shrubs. He died when I was a boy. After his farms and greenhouses were sold, I thought little about flowers. The first books I wrote were scholarly. They were readable and appealing but conventional, their architecture red-brick and Georgian. I did not anticipate drifting from groomed historicism. I lived in libraries and relished spading through forgotten books. I liked seeing my hands and trousers dusty with sloughings from crazed pages. But in my late thirties flowers suddenly appeared. I did not plant them. Like "Naked Ladies" they sprouted overnight, their bulbs gifts from Grandfather. Over the years my books have become progressively bosky. Flowers and trees are so thick on some pages that they appear clipped from garden catalogues. I hoe and curry grammar, but most of the flowers are wildflowers, and my books have become weedy and grabby with scrub. There are few alleys or parterres. Vistas are rough and unsettled, making it easy for readers devoted to narrative regularity to lose their ways. Four years ago a critic said that despite being coiffed by margins and lines my paragraphs were often so natural and thick with cuttings they seemed unnatural.

Although I am often mystified, such remarks don't deflate. On the other hand what boosts my spirit is that Grandfather's love of plants has bloomed in Edward. He is bookish, but he doesn't write on paper. He writes on the ground, his parts of speech, birds, flowers, trees, insects, and reptiles. The spines of all books eventually deteriorate, and pages fall out and are lost. Plantings also disappear. Often, because they are not as forced as books, their moments endure longer, if not on the earth then in the mind. Years ago Vicki and I and the children lived in Perth, Australia. We rented a small house in Mosman Park, a suburb adjacent to Peppermint Grove, Perth's wealthiest district. Gardens in Peppermint Grove were luxuriant. However most plants in them were not indigenous and thus not hospitable to native insects and birds, knowledge Edward brought back to Connecticut.

Along Greenville's Main Street crepe myrtle had been planted, thicker in the south end of town than the north where willow oaks grew. Bushy pink and white, the myrtle shined like early morning. The trees shed their bark, and trunks appeared mottled with gray and blue eventually morphing into muscular creamy orange columns. When I walked down town, the trees blotted awareness of the construction of condominiums just beyond the sidewalk. Crepe myrtle was not native having been brought to South Carolina almost 240 years ago. Despite their being decorative and cheering, Edward disapproved of them and cut down the single crepe myrtle in his yard. For my part I cannot erect a horticultural wall around appreciation. Throughout South Carolina clumps of mimosa or Persian silk tree thrive. Mimosa is an old immigrant, and like crepe myrtle arrived 240 years ago. Some people damn it as a weed tree. If it is a weed, it is one that enriched my childhood and which I have planted on my pages. Three grew outside the kitchen on Cabin Hill, Grandfather's farm in Virginia. They were the only trees I could climb, and morning after morning I scurried up my favorite tree, settled on my perch, and amid a perfumery of pink fragrance and wispy blossoms, listened to cicadas, searched for tree frogs, and kept "my eyes peeled" for snakes.

Edward's yard was unruly. He hadn't clipped and basted the grass with chemicals. As a result, at dusk, a Milky Way of fireflies floated upward. In Connecticut and around the edges of our woods in Nova Scotia, lightning bugs are comparatively rare, so much so that when I notice several, I summon Vicki. During my childhood pesticides had not become a drenching fog, and fireflies were a happy evening sight. Of course, rarely is pleasure unallowed. Battalions of mosquitoes accompanied the fireflies in Edward's yard. The Carolina mosquito is not a diffident anopheles; it a thorax thumping, red-blood sucker capable of driving Karna whimpering to the living room.

Edward's plantings were rigorously native. The railings leading up and around the small porch off his kitchen door were a vinery: Carolina Jessamine light on the eye, after-dinner American Wisteria syrupy and cloying, and Maypop or Passionflower, the blossoms, fizzing, celebratory and electric with blue and silver. The flowers of red trumpet honeysuckle flared in brass sections, their pipes crimson, and bells yellow. Closed blossoms of cross-vine looked like scarlet bags of party favors. Beside the house grew several milkweeds: whorled, swamp, and butterfly bright with orange like the wings of monarch butterflies. The verge was a knee-high hedge of yellow partridge pea. By the front door common milkweed was five feet high. Its leaves were flat green paddles, and its flowers alive with a dither of bees. Hidden amid the leaves and tall stems was a nest box. Inside bluebirds were raising a second hatching. In past years house wrens usurped the box. At various heights throughout the yard Edward placed bird houses to attract migrants and suburbanites. In the tangle of bush in the back of Edward's yard, brown thrashers whistled, chortled, clicked, and trilled, sounding like catbirds. Every year catbirds nest in the forsythia separating my house from the rental property next door. In the afternoon they visit the birdbath in the side yard. Only once had I seen a brown thrasher, and observing several in Edward's yard made me want to sing an uplifting, joyful song like "Oh, Happy Day."

Scattered unobtrusively through the yard were grasses and shrubs. The variety made them eyecatchers: dog hobble, winterberry, butterfly bush, sourwood, hazelnut, little bluestem grass and inland sea oats, the seed heads of this last chevrons stacked and pressed. Across the yard flowers bloomed unpotted: purple spikes of blazing star, rattlesnake master, Indian pinks, gaudy Carolina lilies, beautyberry, its flowers mittens around the stems, silverleaf mountain mint, flowerheads trembling under the weight of bees, vibrating like the bees themselves, and sundry asters and goldenrods, among the latter white leaf goldenrod, a wildflower I hadn't seen before. I drifted across the yard, brushing my hands across the warty corrugated bark of a hackberry and looking at the brush pile of limbs dropped by a water oak, its waywardness welcome after the nervous miles of interstate driving.

For many older people before their knees and backs crumble, place often resembles a greenhouse. Vicki and I are walkers, and our children have not so much followed our footsteps as raced ahead, wandering landscapes too harshly daunting for the us we have become. Edward knew we enjoy the outdoors, and for our pleasure and theirs, he and Erica accompanied by Sammy in an all-terrain baby carriage took us on several outings. Because its football team is good, Clemson has an indifferent academic reputation. The university's standing would grow if the public associated the school with the South Carolina Botanical Garden, 295 acres of gardens veined by trails located on the edge of the campus. We spent a morning walking the gardens, among them, the Hosta, the Camellia, the Aquatic, and then the Natural Heritage Garden. In this last were sections focusing on plants endemic to the Piedmont Woodlands, Longleaf Pine Savannahs, and Mountain Bogs. Most plants in the Children's and Butterfly garden were yard familiars: cleome, zinnias, blue salvia, and broad salvers of candied hibiscus. In the Duck Pond red-eared pond sliders floated near the path hoping passersby would toss treats to them. A luminous green anole scooted along a fence pausing to display the red dewlap under its chin. Our observations were random, the way life is off the page and out of the classroom. Oconee bells opened. Cicadas sang. A towhee whistled then chitted, and a red-shouldered hawk soared overhead while I studied a white pitcher plant, pink veins jittering through it looking like spider webs.

After leaving the garden, we returned to Greenville and ate lunch at a picnic table outside the Swamp Rabbit Cafe. Throughout the visit, I copied signs, sometimes from store windows, other times from the roadside. "Bloom Where You are Planted" seemed good advice, albeit unappealing to nomadic Americans. A sign of the times was "No Concealable Weapons Allowed." "American Made. For Life," read an advertisement for Palmetto State Armory's "9mm AK pistol version of the Russian Vityaz submachine gun." "Have a Blessed Day," Vicki said, repeating the local Holiness spin on "Have a Nice Day." All anecdotes in print are lies, Thomas De Quincey wrote. Certainly whopperish tales appeared in the Greenville newspaper. One morning I read that a woman's husband died during the final ten minutes of a midnight showing in a small movie house in Hickory, North Carolina. On hearing the wife howling, the owner of the theater called the EMT's and paused the film while the technicians removed the body. The EMT's were efficient, and they, their paperwork, the new widow, and the carcass were out of the theater in twenty minutes. Because the movie was exciting and because only a shoot-up and a canoodling finale remained, the owner resumed the showing after "the silent patron" departed. A few customers left during the interval, but most remained. To ease them through the intermission, the owner of the theater treated them to tubs of hot buttered popcorn, soft drinks of their choice (most chose Cokes), and packets of M & M's, though according to the account two teenagers requested Skittles. Under most circumstances I would have guffawed and praised the lie. But the account was probably true. No conscientious anecdotalist would have neglected to mention the name of the film being shown.

A broadside in the window of a hairdresser read like a WOKE pronouncement. "In this Salon, We welcome our guests. We listen to requests. We care about People. We love Hair. We believe in Sustainable Beauty. We celebrate Grace and Eloquence. We appreciate suggestions. We believe that Beautiful is also good." "Is this satire?" Vicki asked me. "Not on your ass," I replied. "We are in a part of town that pretends to be modish." Not every with-it place thrived. Down the block, Eve's Aprés the Apple Boutique had closed. The store's name was likely too recondite for a dress shop. Mistakenly, the owner assumed that that women living in the "Bible Bodice" knew that Eve began wearing clothes only after eating the apple.

A few strides away from our picnic table on a bank above the Reedy and on the property of Mt. Calvary Baptist Church was Bootleg Corner. On this plot of ground in the 1930s-1960s, an historical marker explained, "stood the home of 'Fat Ma.' Her home served for years as a local distribution center for illegal moonshine stilled in the mountains of Marietta and Asheville then cooled and hidden in the nearby Reedy River. Customers in those days frequented the corner for something to satisfy their thirst. Now the property belongs to a ministry offering the living water of Jesus Christ to all who will believe. Jesus said, 'whosoever drinks of the water that I will give him shall never thirst; but the water I will give him will become in him a well of water springing up to eternal life.' John 4:14."

Thirsts change, but since our marriage Vicki's and my thirsts have remained constant. On wet and dry days, in deserts and rain forests, we have walked. Our moonshine has been the living water of life itself, a glimpse of yellow warblers on the wing, the fragrance of sweet pepper bush, or cardinal flowers scarlet amid gravel along the bend of a river. We have only sipped, but although shallow, our draughts have been deep enough. Not all our strolls have been lyrical. But they've gotten more so. They distance us from age and, in Wordsworth's phrase, "what man has made of man." In the woods I don't return to reason and faith as Emerson wrote. I don't become an optimist, but for a moment pessimism lifts. I don't quote Methuselah's favorite remark, "dying is such goddamn hard work." I dream. Frailties dissipate like white mist smothering a field in the early morning. In Greenville I imagined Sammy's budding life, days not gnawed into dregs by social budworms or scarab beetles.

Another morning while Erica worked from home, Edward took Vicki and me and Sammy to Lake Conestee Nature Preserve, some 406 acres of wetland and wood east of Greenville laced with trails and boardwalks. The lake was formed in 1892 when the Reedy River was damned near a mill. Sediment at the bottom of the lake is a sludge of industrial waste too dangerous, and probably too expensive to be disturbed. As a result the lake is a calm eye, its surface not infected by the conjunctivitis of motorized entertainment. On the water and amid the surrounding forest and marshes, birders have identified over two hundred species of birds. For our part we roamed without purpose. Still, our surroundings were rich. Barking tree frogs greeted us or so I thought. At times my hearing is more fanciful than precise. Quickly, I recognized water primrose, arrowhead, and the blue spires of pickerel weed. The bark of a sugarberry tree was warty and in places keloidal. A barred owl played peek-a-boo with us shifting back and forth behind a broken tree trunk. A red swamp crayfish going walkabout raised its pincers. Blue herons and great white egrets hunted in the shallows of the lake. Slaty skimmers do-si-doed along the shoreline while a voracious eastern pondhawk seized a damselfly. River cooters sunned on logs, and organ pipe mud daubers built lyres of nests under the roof of a shelter. The wasps stuff chambers in the nests with paralyzed spiders. On hatching, the larvae eat the spiders. As a boy in Virginia, I opened cells. The large number of black widow spiders amazed me. Indeed much of what I now see brings childhood to mind. At times I inhabit the past more than the present, a state of being, Vicki once said, "typical of the old and atypical for the young." "Commonsensically so," I thought, "because youth hasn't lived as long and lost as much."

Our excursions in Greenville were local and short, suited for aching knees and perhaps gimpy minds. One morning Edward drove us to Asheville, a town of which he and Erica are very fond. Unlike Greenville, Asheville seemed cluttered. Wedges of fretful people clumped uncomfortably together on the curbs of the up and down streets. All seemed eager to be elsewhere. While Vicki bought Sammy a onesie at Spiritex, I sat on a bench at Pritchard Park.

Most people in the park had been mauled by drugs and life's unfairness. By Conestee Lake I felt curious and exuberant. At the park I felt tired, dispirited, and aware of social dissolution. Recently I'd read a statement by a political divine, "the person who pities rogues is the enemy of honest people." But, of course, I thought, "the Sammy a grandfather cradles in his arms doesn't start out to go wrong and probably isn't responsible for how life bends him."

Such thoughts go well with grimy park benches, but not with family lunches, in which the best appetizer the old can serve is joviality. We ate at the Laughing Seed, the first time I ate at a vegetarian restaurant. I drank water, and Vicki a draft pilsner. We split two sandwiches. The ingredients intrigued me. The first sandwich was a Reuben made from house-cured sweet potato pastrami, smoked onions, house purple kraut, Swiss cheese, and thousand island dressing on "Annie's grilled marble rye," the second a curried chickpea salad wrap, "a creamy chickpea salad in a garlic herb wrap" with sriracha slaw, lettuce, tomato, and onion. Were they good? Vicki said they were excellent. Alas, since having the virus the first week in February, my sense of taste comes and goes promiscuously. I tasted neither sandwich much as I didn't taste the "lip-smacking" cod cakes Erica made for dinner one night. Insofar as smell is concerned: I smell flowers and blooming shrubs, but much else is odorless. Two mornings after we returned to Storrs, the town flushed the sewer line outside our house. Vicki said the neighborhood reeked and despite the heat refused to open the windows. I smelled nothing and went outside to watch the work. At the edge of the road a fountain of water shot up when a workman removed a manhole cover. I leaned over to look down the pipe.

"Be careful," the man advised, "you might get hit by a 'floater.'" A floater's smacking my face might have stung, but I wouldn't have whiffed it, no matter where it hit: eyes, ears, nose, mouth, or chinny-chin-chin.

Trips are often calendars of meals and frequently of little else. As benefits the too well-traveled, we ate simply. The sandwiches at Laughing Seed were each fifteen dollars. Including the tip, lunch cost $103.81. During our days in Greenville, Vicki and I paid for all the meals away from Edward's house and for the ingredients of meals we ate there. The most expensive meal cost $235.20 at Passerelle restaurant. We ate dinner on a balcony overlooking Reedy Falls, and the view was better than the food. During the twelve days in Greenville all of us frequently had coffee and muffins at Old Europe Cafe spending a total of $191.53. We tracked our expenses. I spent $143.15 on gas and arrived home with two-thirds of a tank remaining in the car. At Sunshine Sammies in Asheville, I paid $18.02 for ice cream sandwiches. At the Lost Cajun in Greenville a seafood lunch cost $85.36. I had a shrimp gumbo which I couldn't taste. Twice I bought pizzas at Sidewall. They cost $20 a piece, and we took them back to Edward's house and ate them. I drank a bottle of Red Stripe beer. The pizzas were toothsome, especially one dubbed Greenville Goddess. Because my taste suddenly fired on eight buds, I wasn't forced to wash the pizzas down my gullet. I do not know why I tracked expenditures. According to Douglas Jerrold, "money is a habit—nothing more." Jerrold may be right. Resisting the habit in a capitalist country is difficult. Even harder is embracing things that are much more valuable.

Vicki and I tried not to burden Erica and Edward. I never used the bathroom in their house, and after a day's jaunting, we often returned to our hotel early in the evening. We insisted that lunch stuffed us and that we were too full for dinner and only wanted to go to bed. Later we strolled Main Street, purchasing ice cream or beer as the night suited us. The walks were long and relaxed. I delight so much in Vicki that unaccountably the fear that something terrible will befall her suddenly shrouds me with terror and causes the gay moods to droop and mourn. When that happens I don't, as Keats suggests, "glut" my feelings by looking at a rainbow or bushes of peonies. I am not a poet. I eat and eat with Vicki, and as we munch, the indigestion of feelings passes. Twice we ended walks by eating pork at Husk. In Greenville none of Little Betty Pringle's pigs last past early shoathood. They quickly bed down with green beans, collards, and cheddar grits, their slumber couches perfumed by Birds Fly South, a pilsner brewed near Greenville. Edward and Erica don't like pork, and our keeping Husk to ourselves added a palate-titillating spice to the meals, enabling me, I think, to taste everything.

Beside the baseball tee-shirt, the only other items I purchased were books. Because the train of a hurricane was supposed to sweep across Greenville, I planned to read through the rain. The storm went elsewhere. Nevertheless, I read. I bought the books at M. Judson located in the old courthouse downtown. The store's offering of Southern writers was rich with the parochial and literary, books written for read- ers who want reading to be more than time-passing entertainments. I bought two of Kevin Wilson's books, *Baby, You're Gonna Be Mine,* a collection of short stories, and *Nothing to See Here,* a novel. I'd long real- ized that I should read Wilson but had not done so in part because to me he was a "new" Southern writer, not one of the writers whom I'd known and read for years, writers whose books smacked of home, indeed of the familiar life I led and of people recognizable and understandable. Among the many things age separates a person from is the appreciation of newness. I, for example, cannot operate much of the gadgetry in our Subaru and don't intend to learn, "I can drive the sunbitch," I tell Vicki, "and that's enough." Even the rough language I use is dated, "old school," I say thinking the phrase praise but aware that for many people it evokes a blinkered and hidebound past. In any case the phrase is "swell." Once I started Wilson's books, I read deep into the night. What happens to ordinary people and their ordinary lives when three children periodically burst into flame? And are such children themselves ordinary despite being combustible? How could anyone resist reading a story, the first line of which states, "It was almost midnight when my girlfriend got a call from her sister, who had been arrested for taking a kebab skewer at a cookout and stabbing her husband." The only cookout I have been to in fifty years was on July fourth at Edward's house. Edward cooked chicken kebabs. Erica made blueberry gelato; Sammy played with a yellow Lorax Vicki gave him, and no one got stabbed.

In another of Wilson's stories a baby disappears, as in a sense all babies ultimately disappear. "The baby was so beautiful, so perfect," the tale begins, "that Maggie constantly allowed herself the fantasy of eating her baby, of consuming him until the baby was housed entirely inside of her own body. 'You are so beautiful,' she whispered to the baby." Would that Vicki and I could have carried Sammy back to Connecticut with us, could have carried our perfect baby for the rest of our lives. We knew, of course, we'd lose Sammy as years ago we lost our little threesome, Francis, Edward, and Eliza.

We did not pack a meal when we left Greenville. Our only snack consisted of two key lime cookies handed to me at the opening of Byrd's on Main Street, one of a chain of fifteen sweet shops. The cookies freshened a moment, but the drive was acidic. In hopes of avoiding traffic jams, I occasionally took back roads. The number of cars wasn't large; the kudzu sculptures were memorable, but the shoulders of the roads were the only rest stops, gravelly and open-aired. I'd rather kick the wind than make the trip again. At home life fell into the usual pattern. Vicki had her teeth cleaned. I mowed the grass to forestall the spread of ticks, and Amy from Medical Services called peddling a medical alert system. In fact, Amy telephoned five days in a row, taking weekends off. A concerned scammer called twice to warn that our nonexistent Amazon Prime Account had been compromised, and a fund-raiser from my old college Sewanee reminded me that "August is Make-A-Will Month." My cousin Sherry rang from Richmond and inquired about our trip. One night during the previous week, she said, her electricity went off. She used a flashlight to look up the number of Dominion Energy. Sherry is my age. Like her eyes, her flashlight was weak. The number she dialed was one digit off. A recorded message responded to Sherry's call saying, "If you wish to speak to a man, press one. If you wish to speak to a woman, press two." "I almost pressed a number," Sherry said. "I am so used to pressing five or six numbers before I reach a human being—at the pharmacy or the bank. But while trying to decide whether to talk to a man or a woman, I realized I hadn't dialed the power company."

A stranger wrote and said that in a study of "Conformity," he'd quoted a sentence from a book review I scratched out in 1972. "But with imagination, the all-boy boy never fails to dynamite the jail." "Forty-nine years ago!" I said to Vicki. "What jail? I was still wet behind the ears and in the brain." The most appealing letter waiting for me was from Bob White in Perth. Bob has never driven an automobile and for six decades has walked or ridden buses to work. This year, he recounted, "I bought each of my daughters a car. I remain afoot." For years peacocks have lived around and in the courtyard of the Arts Building at the University of Western Australia where Bob taught. New chicks, Bob wrote, were named after recently deceased members of the faculty. "What kind of bird would you be?" Vicki asked. "A turkey buzzard or a great big mother of a marabou stork, one with a gular sack bigger and smellier than an elephant's scrotum." "Not the bluebird of happiness or that candy-striper Robin Redbreast nursing Jenny Wren, not even that irritating little sparrow that goes 'hop, hop, hop' and won't 'stop, stop, stop'?" Vicki said. "Maybe tomorrow," I said. "Right now I am earthbound. Driving has clipped my tongue, and I'm too tired to titmouse around with words."

The morning after arriving home we drove to Pomfret and fetched the dogs. They were ecstatic to see us. They yipped and ran around and through our legs tying us and their leashes into canine love knots. By afternoon, however, arthritic indifference had set in, and they were again sleeping days away. For dinner that evening Vicki and I split a bowl of Drunken Noodles from Fresh Fork. As a side dish we had an ear of corn and a handful of "barbecued" potato chips, neither of which I could taste. In Greenville I came down with my yearly sinus infection. Edward fetched a nasal spray from his medicine cabinet. The expiration date was November 2012. I tried it, and it may have helped a little. Home is where the doctors are, though, and I did better in Storrs. After taking cefuroxime twice a day for ten days the infection dried up.

The doe, the yearling, and the fawn who camped in the woods behind our house were still resident. My picking up sticks did not disturb them. In our absence a groundhog dug a burrow under the clothesline in the backyard. We haven't settled on a name, but we are leaning toward Becky. She is, of course, a vegetarian, Pennsylvania smartweed being the favored appetizer of the moment. An orchard of oak apple galls lay on last year's leaves in the woods glowing and looking like Ferrero Rocher candy wrapped in golden foil. Dame's rocket bloomed, and I was able to smell the sweet peppery fragrance. Rain awakened soft polypore from its spring nap. So many white shell-like brackets suddenly materialized that the trunks of dead trees looked like beaches. Running my hand slowly over the mushrooms made a plunking sound like water dripping from a leaky faucet. When I sped the movement up, the leak became a drizzle. On the campus panicle hydrangeas were mounds of snowballs, and under a weeping European beech, cities of Indian pipes had risen from the ground looking like miniature skyscrapers white in the light of a full moon. Shortly after returning home, I had lunch with Alex, a deaf friend. Alex had lost his hearing aid, and our conversation sounded like members of the Drones Club greeting one another on the British stage, "What? What? Eh what, Old Blot? Strawberry nose! You knobby marrow! What ho! Eh?"

Alex and I are devotees of literary diversity. We prefaced lunch with an Episcopal blessing, "For what we are about to eat, etc. Hand me the potato chips." After dessert we invoked Calliope and quoted verse as inspirational as chocolate. On this occasion, Alex recited four lines from Richard Munkittrick's Romantic "At Dewy Morn." "The flower that seems of the softest silk made / Cradles the bee on the mountain brow; / And out in the sunshine the rosy milkmaid / Adroitly manipulates the cow." We have quoted poetry to each other for years. Humor gets a passing mark, but citing forgotten poets receives "highest honors." Last spring I resuscitated Edward Capern, "The Rural Postman of Bideford." Capern composed poems while delivering mail. Roadside sights or conversations with farm workers suggested subjects. For a desk he often used a stile or a gate to a field. Other times he sat beside a "friendly hedge" and resting his post-bag on his knees "penciled out his thoughts." To celebrate the arrival of June I recited the first stanza of "A Warble": "The balm-breathing hawthorn is blowing again, / The rocks by the road-side are yellow with broom, / The lilac is sweet with fresh summer rain, / And the peasant's white cottage is rosy with bloom." "Our broom being daffodils?" Alex said. "Yes," I answered, "and the cottages, dormitories."

After lunch with Alex, I sent an email to a woman in Iran freeing her from having to pay a fee to translate one of my books. In the correspondence she asked why I became a teacher. "What bumps into a person or what he bumps into shapes his life," I replied writing the moment's simple after-breakfast truth. "I cannot explain how or why I became a teacher. It just happened—happened like the sunrise. One day I was in the classroom, and my life blossomed." I stressed that I had no high intentions. "I wanted students to enjoy reading and their lives. I did not preach or indoctrinate. I told stories, and they told me stories. We read poetry and novels, and in some magical way we were happy and thought we both were learning." Sending an email to distant Tehran made me recall lost memories, among others, riding a camel across Wadi Rum, being eaten by bedbugs on the overnight train from Cairo to Luxor, swimming through a bale of banded sea kraits off Fiji, and drinking myself so silly in Georgia that the KGB (good fellows) escorted me back to my hotel. "Shit," I thought, but didn't say or write, "Did those things happen?"

Edward mailed us a video of Sammy's laughing and picking up a ball and throwing it. He looks like a southpaw. How Vicki and I hated to leave that baby! We'd like to believe he misses us, but we know that is sweet fantasy. While we were in Greenville, days seemed to pass slowly, but in near-sighted hindsight, they appear vibrant and pulsating with light and affection. The hours were so alive that sleeping didn't come easily. Now Vicki and I are somnolent. We dread autumn and the drift of falling leaves then winter and snow and doctors' appointments. Often we talk about the lives Sammy may or may not lead. We talk about the lives our three children may have led and are leading now. We talk and talk. Trees shed dead lichen-encrusted limbs. Sometimes I hear them thump the ground. Becky shuffles across the front yard toward the road. "Please, please watch out for cars," Vicki whispers.

# Reading at Eighty

Four decades ago, I wrote an essay entitled "Reading at Forty." Vicki and I had been married two years. Our son Francis was seven months old, and Edward and Eliza were not yet dreams. I had begun my fourth year in Connecticut. I "loved" teaching and thought the English Department idyllic. We lived on the campus in a small university apartment, surrounded by the families of other junior faculty members, and I had just bought a red Plymouth Reliant station wagon. In great part I bought the car to have a safe vehicle to drive to the airport in Hartford to fetch Mother and Father for whom Francis was years of wishes come true. I was energetic and swam two thousand yards four days a week. Vicki and I were joyous and exuberant, and the essay reflected our happiness. It skipped lightly through time and place and genre, from the sixteenth through the twentieth century, from Connecticut to Nova Scotia, through newspapers, herbals, and novels, children's books and poems. Diminishment did not cloud mood, and I didn't force vibrant disorder into seriousness. I didn't search for truth. In fact, I believed and still believe most truths man-made conveniences imposed as people age and become less flexible. As they tire of questioning and wondering, indeed of living itself, as their minds harden, people demand truths that narrow and chop, that explain, and too often, exculpate. "I'd give anything for a playful dose of Looney

Tunes," my friend Josh said last week after watching the evening news.

In the essay I vagabonded along. I wrote that I did not plan my reading or let it determine the way I lived but instead allowed it to rise out of living itself. I think the statement was partially true. Of course, a rigorously unplanned page would be unreadable. Not only must all writers be vaccinated against heedless spontaneity, but they should administer boosters to themselves every time they are exposed to a pencil. To draw from Wordsworth, only recollecting in tranquility makes thought and emotion page worthy. Obviously that statement is the observation of the person writing "Reading at Eighty." Perhaps half a lifetime ago I would have believed it stuffy and confining. In any case forty ought to differ from eighty. For the record, although I frequently cite them, I don't slavishly genuflect to the Romantic Poets. Coleridge's "the best words in the best order" now seems a militaristic parade ground statement. I prefer smidgens of disorder in uniforms and paragraphs, the random, the out-of-line that makes one notice and question the inline. Lastly, I intend to expand the two essays into a trilogy, the third entitled "Reading at One Hundred and Twenty." Time will determine the content of this last piece, but for interested readers let me announce that I am accepting advances. Moreover, I will get underway soon. My friend Josh advises me "to begin before 2061." No matter the popularity of the trilogy, I doubt I'll write a fourth essay in 2101. Still, some pages of my favorite authors are so long-lived they seem to have been bathed in glutaraldehyde and menthol, for example, the novels of Dickens and Jane Austen. Perhaps during multiple rereadings the chemicals rubbed off on me and have preserved my writing hand.

Reading is more important to American nomads, that is, people living miles away from their childhoods than it is for people settled in the towns in which they went to school. At "home" even amid the solitude of age, memory rarely sinks into lethargy. Anecdotes appoint their days, and associations swell naturally into stories and don't need an infusion of pages to flourish. Reading also matters more to the old than to the young from whom signatures of friends and plots have yet to fall away. That said, although the old have more time to read than when they were youthful, paradoxically they read less. For my part I subscribe to a single periodical, *The London Review of Books*. Many of the articles are heavy going. I refuse to get bogged down, and I trod through them in an evening, high-stepping over mucky thought. The only newspaper I read is the *Willimantic Chronicle*. It is ten or some-times twelve pages long, and the two columns I scan regularly are the obituaries and the list of house sales. Much of the population of eastern Connecticut is old, and the last page of the first section usually focuses on articles that might interest the aged: retirement, sensible investments, and how to bundle a mate into a nursing home without becoming a pauper. I don't read that particular page because according to Vicki I don't have the patience to give "a big goddamn." Because of donations managed by Vicki, we receive a kitchen table of magazines, all-natural history, among others, Cornell's *Living Bird*, *Audubon*, and *National Wildlife*. These arrive irregularly, and I peruse them at breakfast. They make me hunger for a better world, but because they show what man has made and con-tinues to make of Nature, paradoxically they often depress my appetite and sour my mood.

Although I have much leisure, indeed endless

down, boring time, I lack the drive to read great books. My meanderings with Menelaus and Achilles on the plain of Troy ended sixty years ago, and although I recently read and enjoyed Frederic Martyn's *Life in the Legion*, an account of five years served in the French Foreign Legion, looking at *War and Peace* on my bookshelf convinces me I suffer from an enervating autoimmune ailment triggered by hefty volumes. For example, reading the Parliamentary and Barchester novels of Trollope for a third time, as an acquaintance recently suggested, strikes me as Sisyphean, a labor that would cause even the mythological rock-roller to contact his union representative. "Don't retired teachers read so they will have topics to blather about?" an old friend, a naïve banker, asked me. Even in their salad days teachers rarely discussed books, and their best chit-chat appeared in reviews. By the time a person reaches eighty, literary palaver has gone the way of, and actually, seems less significant than gossip. Oldsters talk more about medicine than about books. In fact, I spent a goodly portion of Friday afternoon reassuring a friend about prostate examinations. He'd avoided doctors since childhood and the prospect of an examination horrified him. "They are nothing," I told him. "Just grin and bear it. After a couple of intimacies, you may even grow to enjoy them." His response was all I could have wished for but, alas, unprintable even for someone in a Henry Miller mood.

As far as literary criticism is concerned, "my career," as a former president of a southern university put it, "have done come and went." Moreover, after my death, my children will glance at the books I've written and probably quote the famous funeral poem which begins, "Can this be, that this is all that remains of thee." Incidentally I never used *career* to describe my teaching years. Pompous and tainted by ego, it is aggrandizing and insinuates that individual exertion, rather than luck or, more likely, ordinary living, determined the course of life.

Dress does not make a man, but it can determine how others view him. I taught in a coat and tie. Outside the classroom, I wasn't a suit and clearly wasn't a "careerist" susceptible to the siren song of conforming ambition. I wore shirts on the fronts of which appeared whirls of salamanders or layers of insects, on the bottom of this last beetles gnawing through rotten logs, at the top moths fresh from pupal naps testing their wings. My favorite was the Bat Child shirt, supposedly reprinted from the front page of the *World News*. "Bat Child Found In Cave!" a headline read. Under the heading appeared a picture of the child. He was bald, had googly eyes, pointed ears, and sharp teeth. A scientist said, "His great eyes see in the dark; his ears are better than radar." Whenever I donned the shirt, someone asked where I got it. In the past I told the truth: my son Francis bought it for me. Now I curtsy to a higher morality, that is, I lie, and say the shirt was given to me by a Republican who believed the presidential election was stolen, that the best treatment for coronavirus was horse dewormer, and that sexual intercourse with demons caused miscarriages, especially with demons that have purple horns, three legs, and two pupils in each eye.

Despite teaching three or four classes each semester, and Vicki's and my being the parents of a lively little boy, forty years ago I had more uninterrupted reading time than I do now. In 1981, the telephone rarely rang. Today the phone rings often. On the line are not family or friends but crooks. I don't wear my ears out listening to strident Amy or soft-voiced Kim. It pleases me that people are concerned about the warrantee on my car and the condition of the roof above my head, but I don't fritter hours away chatting to commercial Samaritans. How much moola Joe from the Policeman's Benevolent Association and his cousin Ben from Disabled Veterans pocket after plucking their verbal harps for elderly listeners might startle me, but I don't listen long enough to find out. They and all other members of the Sympathy Orchestra are out of tune with the good and the true. The calls are small nuisances. But they disturb mood and rhythm, and after receiving a couple, I meander off—usually to the kitchen where, if Vicki is not guarding the refrigerator, I am liable to stay for a while. Occasionally a call is a real disturbance and is the stuff of story. Such calls cause me to forget the book I am reading, but since they often entertain, I enjoy them.

Last week I got the scam "hi grandpa" call. My grandson Sammy is nine months old. Of course, I'm a conventional grandpa and think him precocious, but so far Sammy has only said one word, "cat," and I knew he wasn't on the line. However, the man calling had a slight English accent, and I thought he might be my buddy Geoffrey congratulating me on finally becoming a grandfather. Geoffrey and I rowed together at Cambridge and have remained friends since. On hearing the man, I hesitatingly said, "Geoffrey?" "Yes," the man said, "this is Geoffrey." On my noting that he sounded "a little hoarse," the man explained that he was tired. He'd come to Florida to attend the funeral of his friend Stephen who caught the virus and died. "The funeral ground me down."

When I asked about Stephen's identity, the man said I met him once at "the house," adding that he'd be surprised if I remembered him. Conventionally the "hi grandpa" or "hi grandma" spam call comes from a grandson arrested in Florida [Florida is the preferred state] on a minor drugs charge and needs two to three thousand dollars to escape durance vile. "Geoffrey, where do you live?" I asked. "Oh, you know that," the man replied sounding irritated. By now I was alert, and the scent of polecat was in the air.

Although I admired the scammer's ability to spin a tale, I hung up. The call had a beneficial medicinal effect, however. For the past month my blood pressure puddled along at an Assisted Living pace between 110 and 100 systolic and 60 and 50 diastolic. The call was just the boost needed to pump the pressure into normal. The caller must have thought he'd hooked a live sap, rather an almost dead one, because four days later he called back. He used the interval to research my family. This time he was Edward my son calling from Greenville, South Carolina. He explained that understanding him might be difficult. When this Edward rebuked a man who knocked a woman aside and broke into a line at a grocery, the man attacked Edward and smashed his nose. "There was blood everywhere." On my sounding startled, the spammer said, "Didn't Erica [Edward's wife] telephone you? She should have."

The spammer said he was telephoning from the police station. The police were not sure who started the fight. As a result, Edward said he needed me to advance money for bail and to pay a doctor in the local hospital to set his nose. The story was too familiar to be true, and I hung up. I wish I'd stayed on the line long enough to tell the man that if I discovered his identity, I'd chop his balls off and feed them to my Rottweiler. That night I sent the real Edward an email describing the phone call. Waiting for me the next morning was Edward's reply. It was lively and funny. "Hi Pops," Edward wrote. "I did have my nose broken. It wasn't my fault, but the police are involved, and they are blaming me! I can't get out of jail unless I raise $10,000. Please send it soon. I can't stand it in here. They are going to charge me with assault, but I am not to blame. Once I get out, I can begin to clear my name."

In my house monetary matters are rarely the source of dinner conversation. Vicki and I are not parsimonious, but neither are we spendthrifts, and our financial talk has generally focused on dime and quarter spending. Only infrequently have the low finances of our days altered the quiet tenor of living. Still, occasionally, humor has led me to close a volume, not before inserting a bookmark, however. On Friday, Vicki bought a tube of Colgate toothpaste at CVS drugstore. The price was $5.59. Vicki paid $.31. A manufacture's coupon reduced the price by $2. Because the toothpaste was "Face, Hair Care," CVS lowered the price by another $3. "Extrabucks" took off $.20, and "Oral" $.10, leaving the total $.29. The 6.35 % Connecticut sales tax added $.02 to the bill, making the total $.31, a provocative result nudging my funny bone and certainly more interesting than any amount requested by a scammer to bail a naughty grandson out of jail.

There are many types of reading, several of which interrupt the bookish hours I spend in my study. The most disruptive is television reading. Vicki and I never watch a show without turning on the subtitles. Almost always the shows come in segments and are visual equivalents of novels published in weekly or monthly parts in the nineteenth century. Illustrations often accompanied Victorian tales. At their best, caricatures drawn by Phiz (Hablot Browne) or George Cruikshank, have proved more memorable than the stories themselves. Subtitles on television shows are insignificant, except when misspelling or grammatical errors enliven them. Still, the subtitles exist, and when shows collapsed in obtuse visual messes, Vicki and I amused ourselves by tracking illiteracies.

The programs that lure me from the printed page are almost always adaptations of light-hearted books, for example, those by P.G. Wodehouse, James Herriot, and Gerald Durrell, volumes celebrating pigs and mishaps at Blandings Castle, love and animals in Yorkshire, and days of childhood and happy misadventures on Corfu before the Second World War. Vicki's and my taste differ. I refuse to watch violence. Guns-out means I am gone. For her part, Vicki likes the equivalent of dime novels greasy with the untoward, shows like "Breaking Bad" and for a while "The Batchelor" and "Batchelorette." For her mental health, however, Vicki has gone cold turkey on the latter two shows. During an eight-minute segment of "The Batchelor," a lovesick duo used *like* as a filler one hundred and thirty-seven "mind-clotting, throat gagging times, that is, seventeen times a minute or once every three and a half seconds."

In truth, more often than not reading fractures my reading. Plaster of Paris repairs the breaks, but not always immediately. Sometimes I limp for a while. Last month I closed a book and mulled life after reading a poem by Thomas Lovell Beddos. "If there were dreams to sell, / What would you buy?" Beddos asked. "Some cost a passing bell; / Some a light sigh, / That shakes from Life's fresh crown / Only a rose-leaf down." Two days earlier, Edward asked if I'd like to revisit Australia. "Wouldn't that be a dream?" he said. Years ago, I wrote three books describing the times our family spent in Western Australia. We were gushingly happy, and words ripened quickly. If I could buy a dream, I'd travel to Australia and stay several months. But, of course, I'd have to purchase a basket of dreams: good health, a worry-free mind, chronic curiosity, muscles, boundless energy, and a capacity for spontaneous delight. In Vicki's basket would be optimism, joy, and the key to a place to live, somewhere the children would be eager to visit. We'd possess these dreams and many more, all at toothpaste prices. Alas, the passing bell has been silent a long time, I mused, then sighed and telephoned a friend in the hospital. He'd been bedridden for forty-six days and didn't know when he'd be homeward bound. We chatted for twenty minutes, but the connection and his ears were bad, and I don't know what we talked about. The best I could do was make bubbly sounds. "Rose leaves surfing the breeze," I thought when I laid the receiver down.

Much of my present reading leads into cul-de-sacs too pinched to allow me to reverse direction. In *Humor, Wit, and Satire*, a collection edited by Edward Bradley, better and more appealingly known as Cuthbert Bede, appeared a sketch entitled "North and South." Beside a stream in the Chevoits separating Northumberland from Scotland, an English foxhunter met a Gaelic maiden balancing a bucket of water on her head. "Can you tell me which way the hounds have gone my good girl?" the Gentleman from the South asked. "Weel, my cannie Southron," the Lady from the North replied. "A vast have ganged through the burnie, and a vast have ganged adoon the brae, and haflins doon the howes by yon yowe-fauld, and haflins by the birks ayont the muir, and syne a few ower the histie stibble." "Oh! thank'ee," the hunter replied, a response that evoked hiccupping laughter—from me at least. "Why is that funny?" Vicki asked. "Oh, Lord! I can't explain," I said, whacking my knees with the palms of my hands. "Peculiar," Vicki said. Vicki herself is the author of the oddest "manuscripts" I read. At breakfast she slices a banana in two. She eats one half and puts the other half in the refrigerator. Because I graze carelessly across the shelves in the refrigerator and sometimes have eaten her banana, Vicki writes her name on the skin. As a result, I read fruits before I eat them, not simply bananas, but also apples and peaches to which she attaches bits of paper on which she writes "VICKI." The papers are small, but to accommodate my aging eyes the letters are large.

Some cul-de-sacs aren't dead ends. Instead of blocking thought, they force reading into unforeseen directions. Learning that Adam and Eve were once conjoined back-to-back, making carnality impossible, well, unlikely, thus keeping earth's human population low and increasing the hospitality of the planet to animals spurred me to ponder the marriage ceremony's "let no man put asunder." Separating Adam and Eve probably was the source of man's enmity to animals. Before the division when a wild creature pursued the couple, Adam could fall to his stomach. Leaning over his arms and using his hands as another pair of feet, he could then gallop on what were essentially four legs. When tired, he rolled over to recuperate, allowing Eve to run on her four "feet." Because Eve was fresh, animals could not keep up with the couple, and if an animal did draw close, rolling over would re-engage Adam's rested legs. Two sets of four legs are faster than one. Unfortunately, once Adam and Eve were separated they slowed. Eventually they learned that culling creatures increased their chances of survival. From killing animals to eating them was a short step, this likely brought about by a bolt of lightning which cooked a newly harvested animal. Later came garlic and all the condiments popular with cannibals.

I've always scoffed at the ancient story that Adam and Eve had furry bodies, bushy tails, scampered up trees, and looked more like squirrels than present-day homo sapiens. Once they abandoned their lodgings in the Tree of Knowledge of Good and Evil, there were certainly plenty of trees in which "our first ancestors" could nest: among others, ancient olives, holm oaks, the cedars of Lebanon, Aleppo pines, and cypress "its upper limbs stretching above Mount Sion and pressed together in prayer." Still, the soil of much of the Holy Land was gritty and sandy, not offering good purchase for the feet of squirrels, making them susceptible to "wild beasts." Of course, my friend Josh opined, "Humans evolved rapidly. They shimmied down from trees. Their claws became finger and toenails. They built huts out of mud and wattle and grew sheep for food. They carved self-help tablets and drafted codes of meritorious behavior. Then they worshipped themselves, invented guns and bombs, and became their own worst predator."

As a person ages, he grows indifferent to Longfellow's declaration that life is real and earnest. At eighty such "numbers" are truly mournful. Cheerleading urging strenuous up and thinking, pursuing and achieving, nauseates me like over-eating. What attracts me are the sides of reading, marginal things in and about books that entertain, sometimes startle, and don't lecture like graduation speeches. Recently many books I read were published near the beginning of the twentieth century. I bought them at used bookstores never paying more than ten dollars a volume. I enjoy holding hand-worn books, perhaps as a bricklayer likes running his fingers over the rough bricks used two hundred years ago as ballast in sailing ships or as a stonemason likes looking at walls raised on hard-hewn massive granite blocks. I realize writing is ephemeral, but handling old books cajoles me into believing the time I spend writing is more than a selfish indulgence. Quickening use soils. Occasionally I imagine a reader's endowing my books with life by tearing pages, scribbling across margins, or spilling tea or coffee on end papers. On my desk is a handful of scraps. Most are bookmarks I found in used books. For me they don't mark ends but beginnings, not the conclusion of a person's reading but the start of a story depicting life beyond the page. The most recent marker I found is a hundred and ten years old. It is the right hand corner of an advertising flyer. Printed on one side of the scrap is the date 1910 and "5 Cents A Copy." On the reverse appear the words "Hamilton Coupons" and "Every grocer." In 1910 Hamilton Profit Sharing Coupons could be used to purchase many items, including Argo Starch, My Wife's Salad Dressing, Peter Cooper's Gelatin, and Runkel's Breakfast Cocoa. Many of the used books I purchased were inscribed. Mazie gave *Cowardice Court* to Georgia in 1907. As I examined the scrap I thought about Mazie and Georgia. Did they buy Bufceco Oats and Golden Egg Macaroni with Hamilton Coupons? Were they good housekeepers and washed their clothes with Swift's Pride Soap?

Perhaps they began using Swift's only after Georgia attended the Allentown Fair in Pennsylvania and sent Mazie a postcard reading, "All the really pretty white dresses at the Fair were washed with Swift's Pride Soap. Everybody here in Allentown uses it."

No scribbler can be certain about the accuracy of everything that he puts on the page. At times he must trust intuition or as in my case habits forged by years of academic research. Adding credence to a favorable assessment of my skills is a card in the study wishing me "All the Best" and signed by Lieutenant Joe Kenda, the "Homicide Hunter" of actual and television renown. A reader of my essays and a friend of the sleuth had the card inscribed and sent to me. Vicki framed the card and set it on a shelf atop an advertisement for Hamilton Coupons she discovered in a junk shop. Published by Buffalo Cereal Company, the ad stated that the coupons would be accepted until January 1, 1914.

Mazie lifted her remark about Allentown and the white dresses from the advertisement Vicki found. Indeed, advertisements are another source of extrabookish pleasure. "CREAMOL For Consumption, Coughs & Colds. Chronic Asthma or Bronchitis, and other complaints of the CHEST, THROAT and LUNGS," declared a page attached to the conclusion of a pulp novel published in 1890. "Unequaled for restoring the system after an attack of Influenza. CREAMOL Conquers Debility and Wasting Diseases of all Kinds. Makes Weak Children and Delicate Women FAT, STRONG & HEALTHY." Even better, Creamol was "Sweet and Pleasant to Taste." Perhaps Creamol also moderated Complaints of the Head. This morning I got out of bed early and came downstairs. I laid shorts, underpants, socks, and a shirt on a chair in the study. I planned to change into them after doing a few small chores. When the time came to put the clothes on, I fetched them quickly, but I could not find my pajamas. I didn't want to leave the pajamas lying around. I wanted to hang them on a rack upstairs. I searched the downstairs, going into every room, looking on the floor and on the backs of chairs. Eventually I asked Vicki if she had seen them. "You are joking, aren't you?" she said. I was wearing the pajamas.

"Yes, of course," I said. "I'm joking." However, in case the medical joke was on me, I intend to place the address of Peter Robinson, owner of the Family Mourning Warehouse atop my will. Robinson sold racks of mourning gear: among others, widows' caps and skirts and mantles "trimmed handsomely with crape." Robinson shipped parcels to "all parts of the United Kingdom." World trade has grown since the advertisement was published in 1857, and Robinson probably now ships to the United States. The Warehouse was located in London on Oxford Street. If the business moved, it would certainly be to another prime and easily discovered location. Because of population growth, the number of potential and actual corpses has increased making the possibility that Robinson is still in business almost a certainty.

Since supplying Vicki with the address of the Warehouse, I have learned that losing track of pajamas is not a cause for worry. It is a sartorial misadventure common among elderly males, no more serious than putting underpants on backwards. As I have aged into my final medical years and every morning wash down a handful of mystery tablets, I read a great deal about Aesculapian matters. Because their "numbers" are silly, not only do the accounts delight but they invigorate. How useful to know that the best way to treat "The Falling Evil" is to harvest skulls—those of deer, bear, racoon, opossum, indeed of any animal, found in wood or field, and if possible, human skulls, these often discovered pushing through lilies at the border of a graveyard. The skull themselves are not useful and are in effect pill bottles. What is medicinal is the moss growing inside the skulls. After extracting the moss, the recipe instructs, wash it in spring water and dry it in the sun. Afterward grind it into a powder and "season to taste." A testimonial opined that the best seasoner was sugar, the second best, shredded rhubarb. Perhaps even more useful is the knowledge that the best way to loosen the tongue of a reticent husband is to place a toad over his heart when he is asleep. Shortly afterward "Old Okra Trousers" will talk and expose his secrets. On waking the following morning, he will not recollect revealing anything. The remedy does not suggest how to dispose of the toad. For my part I'd recycle it and release it in a fallow field.

Many remedies are fillers appearing in anthologies and at the ends of pages. I read them because most of my present doings are fillers—of a different sort but fillers, nonetheless. Actually, the pages of all lives are composed of fillers although many people don't recognize the fact until they're eighty. Not long ago I came upon a column in an old magazine entitled, "Want Places." At the top of the list was "As Snake-Charmer in a Serious Family.--A native, recently converted by the missionaries, from Timbuctoo. No objection to look after a camel, and make himself generally useful." The advertisement probably attracted me because I've long written about snakes and camels. At my desk shadows of vanished Sam

Pickerings hover over my shoulder selecting books and turning pages. I lived two years in the Middle East, and when I stumble across paragraphs describing life in the Levant, my reading slows, almost as if my eyes are trudging through desert sands. Recently I read about a Syrian merchant who travelled between Damascus and Aleppo and Mecca. One day while returning to his home near the Umayyad Mosque, he stopped under a palm and began eating a meal. When a poor Bedouin saw him and asked to share the meal, the merchant asked the man a litany of questions, beginning with "where have you come from?" "I have come from your house," the Bedouin replied. "Well, then," the merchant said, "how fares my son Ahmed?" "He grows in health and innocence," the Bedouin answered. "Good," the merchant replied then inquired, "how is his mother?" "She is free from the Shadow of Sorrow," the Bedouin reported. When asked about the merchant's "beauteous camel" and the dog that guarded his gate, the Bedouin said that the former was sleek and fat, and the latter alert and on the mat by the door.

The answers satisfied the merchant, and he resumed eating without offering a morsel to the Bedouin. Presently a gazelle raced by causing the Bedouin to sigh. On the merchant's asking what provoked the sigh, the Bedouin said, "if your dog had not died, he would not have let that gazelle run past us." "What?" the merchant said, "is my dog dead?" "Yes, he died from gorging himself on Camel's blood." "Camel?" the merchant asked. "Thy camel was slaughtered to furnish the funeral feast of your wife," the Bedouin recounted. "Is my wife dead, too?" the merchant moaned. "Her grief for Ahmed's death was so great she smashed her head against a rock," the

Bedouin said. "Ahmed?" the merchant asked. "He died when your house collapsed and crushed him," the Bedouin said whereupon the merchant rent his robe, cast dirt on his head, and started for Damascus forgetting his meal which the nomad ate believing food shouldn't be wasted.

On being asked why he walked the same road every day, Richard Jefferies said, "I do not want change; I want the same old and loved things, the same wild flowers, the same trees and soft ash-green, the turtle doves, the blackbirds." "Let change be far from me," he implored; "that irresistible change must come is bitter indeed." Forty years ago, change attracted me. Now I resemble Jefferies. In reading, exploration is the province of the young and unformed. I roam old roads and old genres. The wayside nouns and verbs may be different, but subjects are familiar. I particularly enjoy spotting traces of myself amid the wildflowers of fields and years. In George Singleton's collection of short stories, *You Want More*, Curt earned a living as a freelance indexer. The job was mechanical drudgery until Curt began tossing spanners in the works, under "Idiotic behavior" listing every page of the three books on which he was working and then under "Rational thought" citing his name. Curt's actions are common academic conduct. At least one academic of my acquaintance behaved similarly. Tinkering with footnotes and citing nonexistent experts keep teachers alive. Such actions blow quickening breezes through dead linoleum classrooms. Moreover, they make teachers more tolerant and kinder to students who purposely avoid small gates and stray from straight and narrow paths. Memories are fallible, but perhaps a few teachers whom classes taught to value the risible as much as the respectable will remember their former colleague, the professor who wrote thirty-odd books into each of which he inserted fictitious references. Toward the end of his "run" he became freer and more creative and enlivened appendices with nonexistent verse. "Stripping the play out of a scholar," he said, "will at best produce a Communist and at worst a moralist."

The books I now read are not dissimilar from those I read forty years ago. However they affect me differently. Instead of challenging my thought as they once did, they confirm it. In *Pen Sketches* Mortimer Collins observed that "we have all felt the Bohemian instinct. The most respectable of elderly gentlemen, punctual as to his dinner-hour, and proud of his unquestionable port, can remember the time when the vagrant and irregular tendency was strong upon him." More than in the past I enjoy pages that celebrate vagrant moods, a book, for example, like William Beckford's *Biographical Memoirs of Extraordinary Painters* which I read early this month. The painters and their works did not exist off page. Even the genealogies of their families were fictions. The mother of Sucrewasser of Vienna, Beckford wrote, "was the daughter of a Lombard pawn broker, was the best sort of woman in the world, and had no other fault than loving wine and two or three other men beside her husband."

Self is more clearly at the center of my reading now than it was years ago, probably because my life is more restricted and possibilities are fewer and less appealing. Recently I read Douglas Jerrold's "The Barber's Chair." Typically for someone my age, it confirmed rather than undermined thought. Nightflit entered Nutt's shop and asked him if there were any news. "Nothing," Nutt replied. If an earthquake swallowed London, Nightflit responded, you'd say "there's nothing in the paper." "The fact is, Mr. Nighflit," Nutt explained, sounding like me if some morning Vicki asked about the news while I was munching Grape-Nuts. "I've had so much news in my time," Nutt stated, "I've lost the flavor of it. Couldn't relish anything weaker than a battle of Waterloo now. Even murders don't move. No, not even the pictures of 'em in the newspapers, with the murderer's hair in full curl, and a dress coat on him."

Recently I read advertisements in a college magazine for Tulip Field, Waverley, and Pine Sap, all "adult communities." No advertisement was flammable enough to "light my fire" as one notice put it. Not even the prospect of a visiting podiatrist made me kick up my heels. My reaction would have been livelier had I'd seen a reprint of a two-hundred-year-old ad for "The Palms, Peckham." The Palms offered "all the comforts of home" and the opportunity to "live life to its fullest." In fact, The Palms was a "Delightful Family Residence," consisting "of six rooms (all snake-proof), flat roof, with veranda; capable of making up five beds, stable for two camels, hippopotamus sty, ostrichry, and slave shed, and usual offices." It did not offer on-site care services, but a little more unplanned reading would enable me to recommend an apothecary skilled in the spiritual and physical needs of oldsters. A phrenologist and a cabinet of aperients should suffice.

Although my reading is unplanned, I am no longer flexible, and I resemble Jefferies. Consciously and unconsciously, I read the sorts of books I read four decades ago. Not long ago I read Connie May Fowler's novel *Sugar Cage*. Reason doesn't adequately explain reasons. Each year I read a few books set in the South. I read them because I was once Southern.

Now I am a different person from a different place. However, I always hope to a find a tag describing the Tennessee in which I grew up and which will awaken fond associations. I am not successful, but neither am I disappointed. Fowler's novel is set in Florida, and some chapters occur in fields of sugar cane, others amid hot dark swamps. Perhaps it is impossible for an eclectic eighty-year-old not to discover himself in after-paragraph moments. The day after I finished *Sugar Cage*, Vicki and I roamed the university's Spring Valley Farm. The day was temperate. The sky was a high light blue with only a few clouds floating through it like pinguecula spots. We ambled quietly along a dirt road. On both sides corn leaned into the sun above us. The ears were hard, and the tassels dry and black. When a breeze stirred the air, the corn didn't rustle so much as start to rustle then reconsider. I looked for signs of raccoons, but I didn't notice any broken stalks. Fowler's swamps and the corn field were vastly different. I saw no snakes and heard no mosquitoes. After the walk I didn't peel off leeches. Yet, for a while as Vicki and I walked I was a boy roaming places I hardly remembered, the recollections somehow triggered by the convergence of Fowler's novel and a New England cornfield. "Isn't that a little fey?" Vicki said when I attempted to explain the strangely similar effects of reading descriptions of a dark swamp and ambling through a green field. One of the dangers of academic life is that it encourages explaining the inexplicable. Not understanding is the sire of many things—creativity, foolishness, impudence, delusion, enthusiasm. Sometimes it's better to shrug and continue to stroll along the old road.

I still read novels. Most are older than *Sugar Cage* which appeared thirty years ago. Usually I discover them by happenstance, but sometimes I ferret them out as I did *The Life and Adventures of Valentine Vox, the Ventriloquist* written by Henry Cockton and published in monthly parts beginning in 1839. If I had been able to throw my voice, I never would have quoted nonexistent experts. Disrupting town or faculty meetings with a few properly enunciated quacks and squeals would have satisfied me. In particularly stuffy gatherings, kicking up my hocks and giving voice to a few purebred whinnies would have delighted me. Ventriloquists believe in the unities of the ridiculous, and if sportsmen, conclude their performances with the foxhunting cry "Yoiks! Tally Ho!" However often when a ventriloquist starts something, ends are ends in word or phrase only. At the conclusion of a meeting, a ventriloquist might bring out his French horn or break into "cocoriko," the cry of an escapee from a voodoo ceremony of the sort mentioned by Fowler.

For the aspiring madcap, Vox is a good role model. Once he mastered his skill and became a real semiotician, Vox enlivened the debate in the House of Commons and punctuated deferential whispers in the British Museum. On quiet streets magisterial women dropped their pretentions and grabbing their skirts scampered when they heard "Mad Dog." On a coach, Vox imitated a woman with a baby who "sobbed, and squalled, and coughed, and hooped, and strained, and held his breath." The driver begged the woman to keep the baby quiet. A gentleman riding on the box said the baby was teething. The driver disagreed and said, "it only wants the breast," whereupon the woman said, "I can't keep it quiet. It ain't no use. I must throw it away." A shriek followed soon after, halting the coach and delighting present-day readers who have endured long airplane flights sitting near caterwauling infants. As Vox aged, he tempered his playfulness, and the *Adventures* became a three-decker novel paunchy with stolen children, contested inheritances, mentholated greed, sinister henchmen, kidnappings, confinements in private lunatic asylums, lachrymose love affairs, weedy family trees, and, of course, virtue thwarted but eventually rewarded. The book ended with most good characters saved and beatific in the Promised Land of sentimental novels. Vox himself became "exceedingly wealthy" enabling him "to do an immense amount of good." Never did he permit "an opportunity for the exercise of that power to escape him. The more happiness he imparted to others, the more happy he felt." His acquaintances all esteemed, honored, and loved him. "With his beautiful, devoted Louise [wife], his sweet children, his good mother, his Uncle John [bachelor, benefactor, and benevolist] "who was always in a state of rapture, and seldom indeed, whether at home or abroad, without a child upon his knee," Vox lived "in the purest, enjoyment of health, wealth, honor, and peace." When there is "peace in the valley" and Jesus is a good friend, when one has shaken hands with "Mother again," I suppose the sensible should leave creativity to the Great First Cause. Still, I imagine the temptation to interrupt angelic palaver with "pooh, pooh," "Blarney," or an elongated "Charge" accompanied by the trumpet of Judgment Day would be damn-near overpowering.

Many novels I read now are old and forgotten. They are baggy. Their narratives sag, and their plots drift into digressions. They are like my life and the lives of most old people. Moreover the contents resemble my books, subjects here one month, over there and far away the next. If a person is fortunate, his life is a four or five decker, sprawling through years then after "The End" bound in vellum, his name tooled in gold on the spine. While reading, I copy paragraphs. My interest is momentary, but so is life no matter the number and contents of its pages, not something I said to the unweaned youngsters who once attended my classes. After traipsing through Vox's life, I was in a biographical mood and read Frank E. Smedley's *Lorimer Littlegood, Esq* "a young gentleman who wished to see life and saw it accordingly," a novel published in the mid-1850s. "People who resolve to see life—to know the world, and so forth," Smedley cautioned, "generally start on their expedition with the idea that they are going to have a pleasant voyage. No doubt they calculate on a few foul winds, an occasional collision, and a loose linch-pen or two, but such trifles weigh but slightly with the *agrémens* of travel. How different is the reality! There is little picturesque, entertaining, or pleasing in any sense to be found in the life journey."

"After the first charm of novelty has worn off and the traveler sees things in their proper light, instead of through the spectacles of curiosity and surprise, and by degrees weariness and disgust creep upon him, he is tired of the turmoil and out of humor with his fellow-travelers. He has found the world less good, less wise, and less amusing that he expected it, and he is far from satisfied with the part he himself has played in it. The journey is over. He takes to his bed, thinks how much better he might have employed his time, knows that it is too late, turns his face to the wall and, yes, the journey is over." Smedley was right, but why fret? The wise go to school in the graveyard and learn from the dead. Corpses put up with a lot, both above and under the ground, but rarely do they complain.

Book journeys began for me before first grade. I lay on the living room floor and studied atlases. Soon after learning the alphabet, I began trying to read travel books. Pictures came first, but words followed soon afterward. I rode a hobby horse, not simply to Banbury Cross but across the signatures of pages to see what "Sammie" could buy, among other things as the cries of London suggested, "A penny white loaf, a penny white cake, / And a two-penny apple pie." I read backpacks of travel books when I was forty. No foul winds shredded their pages. I haven't stopped reading them, and my interest in their journeys continues unabated. Sometime during the years between forty and eighty, I wrote accounts of my own travels. When I go to bed, even though it's late, I switch on the light sitting on my bedside table and turn my face to a travel book. In one of his books, *Hot Countries*, Alec Waugh wrote that it was "not easy to break oneself of habits." After spending two years wandering the Pacific and the Caribbean, Waugh returned to London and signed a seven-year lease on a flat in Chelsea. Three months later the flat was in the hands of a house agent, and Waugh was planning to travel to Martinique.

In his *Traveler's Tales* Henry Cadwallader Adams wrote, "There is an old proverb which says, 'travelers see strange things,' meaning that they profess to have seen things, which a wise man will think twice before he credits." Gulliver had many startling, barely creditable, experiences in the "Remote Nations of the World" as did Bunyan's Pilgrim traveling "From his World To That which is to come." I admire, to use Isaac Disraeli's phrase, "ingenious garniture." But in Storrs I have never spotted a Roc or a Kraken. I've never met a Monster with scales "like a Fish," wings "like a Dragon," and feet "like a bear," not to mention fire and smoke billowing from his belly. Light bouncing off the copper wings of a Simurgh hasn't made me blink. I haven't observed a mother snake resuscitate a baby flattened by an automobile by prying its mouth open and forcing morning glory blossoms between its jaws. Bark on the trees in my backyard isn't wool, and Vicki doesn't harvest it to make my clothes. Instead, she buys my garb online, and UPS delivers them not the Huma Bird. Still, when thinking about trips I once took, I always recall odd events, some of which may not have occurred.

Pigs dream of becoming bacon after death, and Christians, angels. My dreams are unexceptional until I think about traveling. Unlike Waugh I don't turn my house over to a real estate agent and leave town, but on pages I see different and entertaining things, some of which seem so fanciful that I don't credit them. Escaping conscious belief if only for a signature of pages simultaneously relaxes and invigorates. The two travel books I've bought recently are Fred Birchmore's *Around the World on a Bicycle* and Colin Thubron's *The Amur River Between Russia and China*. Thubron has written ten additional travel books, all of which I admire. Now eighty-two, Thubron is the best English travel writer of my generation. His wanderings are bruising and adventuresome, and his accounts learned and well-written. Occasionally, in a gray moment when desire obscured reason, I closed a volume, say, *Journey into Cyprus* or *In Siberia*, and indulged the delusion that if I had not been domesticated, if I had not always been so at ease in the world, I might have written better books.

Francis Bacon was wrong. As much as reading makes a full man, it can delude the person whose days have been bountiful into thinking he hasn't lived. According to the *Daily Mail*, when asked his idea of "Holiday Hell," Thubron replied, "Going on a cruise liner." Newspaper interviews are notoriously inaccurate. I have been misquoted more than I have been quoted accurately. Nevertheless, when I read Thubron's supposed response, I gulped. I did not cruise until years after writing "Reading at Forty." I went as a lecturer sailing for two weeks from Cairns and visiting Papua New Guinea. Vicki and the children accompanied me. With me as a public headliner, I thought days were bound to be boringly bourgeois. I was wrong. We had a fine, even exciting, time. I've since spent more than four hundred days of my life on cruise ships. I enjoyed the jaunts and have written a two-decker volume describing my smooth-sailing adventures. Happily, in my life, gulping moments have the lifespan of a mayfly. Vicki calls me to dinner. Suzie rubs her nose against my calf letting me know she needs to go outside, and Edward sends me a picture of Sammy and him sitting in a big brown armchair. Edward is sunny with laughter and love, and Sammy gazes up at him adoringly. "Oh, Lord," I mutter and look out the study window, not seeing but flush with feeling.

First published in the late 1930s and reprinted by Georgia in 2020, *Around the World* describes Birchmore's cycling from Norway to Saigon in 1935 and 1936. Birchmore traveled through some of the most forbidding and dangerous places on the earth. He should have died innumerable times. As a testimonial to his achievement his bicycle is now in the Smithsonian. Fitness, intelligence, mechanical skills, curiosity, a remarkable good nature, capacities to understand and appreciate, and luck, which should never be discounted, kept him alive and cycling. Birchmore described parts of the Levant where I lived in the 1970s and 80s. At that time they were safer and more hospitable. Birchmore also described places I imagined going but visited only as I read *Around the World* and followed his wheel tracks.

Books influence my dreams. Shortly after Birchmore encountered dens of poisonous snakes, I did the same. One night a knot of massive brown vipers rolled out from under a ledge and untying themselves from one another began sidewinding toward Vicki and me. Their skin looked like the tread on a car tire, angular, grooved, and seizing the ground as they grabbled toward us. We couldn't hop a bicycle built for two and scoot to safety, so I behaved like I usually do on confronting danger after midnight. I woke myself. Four nights later I dreamed about the two-headed moccasin that soft-shelled Episcopalians claim seduced Eve in Eden. Orthodox Methodists maintain the serpent was a hoop snake. When Eve dropped the apple core and heisting up her imaginary skirts ran and tried to hide from the site of her peccadillo, the snake pursued her. He seized his tail with his mouth and turning himself into a wheel rolled after her faster than the chariot that swept up Elijah and toted him off to heaven in a whirlwind. Part of the attraction of *Around the World* may stem from my still biking at eighty. My excursions are short. I only peddle to the university library or to the pool at the community center. Although some bright morning I'll bicycle away, my journey isn't over. Reckless student drivers are the single danger. Once a driver caused me to fall and break my arm, However I have not faced Birchmore's king cobras, storms, outlaws, exotic ailments, tribal and religious prejudices, wars, mountains impossible for a trapeze artist to cross, raging rivers, tigers, deserts—a comic book of challenges that would defeat even the great Doc Savage.

In *The Sea and the Jungle* H.M. Tomlinson stated that "he who goes travelling should leave his self at home, or as much of it as is not wanted on the voyage. It is surprising to find how little you want of yourself. The ideal traveler would venture out merely as a disembodied thought, or, at most, an eye." *The Sea* was published in 1920, and the journey Tomlinson described occurred a decade earlier. Much has changed. A hundred and ten years have passed. Most travel is domesticated, and travelers of my generation differ greatly from those described in books whose pages have browned and crazed. For my part I don't try to escape myself. I do not become disembodied thought either when I am traveling or when I read about travel. I don't know if jettisoning the self is better than shouldering it and allowing, encouraging, it to impose itself upon days and thoughts. In truth I don't know what is possible. The self may be only a frail construct, a convenient frame on which to hang sentences. In any case no matter where I am or what I am doing, some version of me is always present.

At times I hanker to read a mesmerizing, picaresque book punctuated by trips around Storrs to Price Chopper and CVS, Dog Lane Café, The Head Husky (a barber shop), Blaze Pizza, Wing Express, and Gansett Wraps. I've mentioned these places in essays. But they are eat-a-day household names, and I lack the skill to make them alluring. If closely examined, the commonplace can become—exotic. If it becomes too familiar, however, it reverts to being commonplace. Moreover, I'm too old to live through "what if's." Better to explore the maze of recollection safely with a book in hand. In *The Sea and the Jungle* Tomlinson traveled on a tramp steamer up the Amazon, his journey inexplicably making me recall sailing from England to New York on a tramp student ship fifty-five years ago. On board was a lanky Dutch girl. I intended to spend the summer working at a boys' camp in Maine, and she was on the way to a girls' camp thirty miles away. We talked often and smiled a lot although we had trouble understanding each other. "A roamer is she," Barry Cornwall wrote describing a grape vine, "And sometimes very good company." Before people began confusing me with an evangelist, I sometimes jumped the rails of respectability and conventional sense. One night near the end of the trip I implored the captain to marry us. The girl was willing, but the captain was not. What if? Thank goodness, I often think, that for forty-five years, I haven't sung, "I won't go home in the morning. I won't go home in the morning. I won't go home in the morning 'till daylight doth appear." One of the miseries of being a comic writer, Horace Mayhew said is "being suspected of doing all the blackguard, out-of-the-way outrageous, improbable, impossible, stupid things you describe." The statement remains true after *comic* is excised and remains as accurate when a scribbler is eighty as it was when he was forty.

"My plan is to have no plan," Alec Waugh explained. "I have written as I have travelled." Except when preparing classes, researching academic topics, and nine months in the mid-70s when I read almost nothing aside from classical literature, I did not rigorously plan my reading. During that exceptional time in the 70s I lived on a third-floor walkup in London. I rarely talked to others and missing the sobering effects of conversation suffered tinges of viral ambition. In the worst of the fever, I told myself reading was laying a foundation which would support me when I achieved some unarticulated high position. After I left the walkup and once again roamed the sidewalks of life and libraries, the delirium disappeared and never recurred. I married Vicki and taught freshman English. I put Plutarch, Thucydides, Cicero, and Livy high in the bookcase and from a low shelf pulled worm-gnawed novels, one of the first of which was George Barr McCutcheon's *The Hollow of Her Hand*. Early in the book, a socialite Mrs. Rowe-Martin appeared wearing black. She had suffered "a recent bereavement," McCutcheon wrote, "in the loss of a four-thousand-dollar Airdale who had stopped traffic in Fifth Avenue for twenty minutes while a sympathetic crowd viewed his gory remains." The Airdale "was given a most impressive funeral and was buried in pomp with all his medals, ribbons, tags, collars, and platinum leashes, but minus a few of the uncollected parts of his anatomy. While it had been a complete catastrophe, he was by no means a complete carcass." "Yes," I said and laughed. Good healthy enjoyment had returned. This spring I resuscitated the novel and reread the section describing the Airdale's "unfortunate passing" to Vicki. Vicki is a Pentecostal creature lover, and I suspected she wouldn't appreciate the excerpt. I was right. "Jesus, Sam," she said, "you're a piece of work." "A piece most of the parts of which are worn out," I thought, "but thanks to pharmacology, one that keeps turning pages and stumbling along."

Those London months aside, during my early and middle years I read all kinds of stories, science fiction, folklore, romance, realism, and comedy. Usually, my interest in a particular genre eddied after a decade and I'd raised a berm of books. I read volumes of narrative verse but rarely love poetry. "If you loves I, as I loves you, / With an affection strong and true" etc., seemed an adequate romantic beginning, and indeed ending. Much poetry I read was summertime verse light on eye and mood. The poems brought a quick smile and like many pleasant things a quicker forgetting. Typical was the first stanza of "Chit Chat." "Pretty little damsels, how they chat, / Chit chat, tittle tittle tat, / All about their sweethearts—and all that; / Chit chat, tittle tittle tat. / Up and down the city how the little damsels walk, / And of the beaux and fashions how the little damsels talk, / And now and then a little bit of slander's no baulk / To their chit chat, tittle tittle tat."

During my childhood years when I studied atlases, I began reading the Hardy Boys mysteries. I explored cabin island and learned what happened at midnight. I swam across the hidden harbor, scaled Skull Mountain, and opening the secret panel climbed into the attic of the house on the cliff. There beneath a disappearing floor I discovered the twisted claw. I was a schoolboy Birchmore. The sinister signpost and the secret warning did not deter me. Unfortunately, not receiving a share of the tower treasure was probably the source of my endlessly imagining melted coins and buying weekly lottery tickets. Nevertheless, while the clock ticks, I have a chance to find the hidden gold. Perhaps it is not in the state treasury but is buried in the lost tunnel or sealed in the hub of the water wheel at the old mill.

The boy with a book by his bed was the father of the man with a mystery on his desk. Until ten years ago, I read great numbers of mysteries and crime novels. Then I stopped. The books became so violent that I began changing the narratives in my dreams, in the process brushing calm sleep aside and so tiring myself that I woke yawning. Occasionally I still read a Victorian or Edwardian detective story, the pages of which are not so clotted with blood and scabbed over by acts of unspeakable brutality. In February I read an omnibus volume containing eight tales by Fergus Hume, *Miss Mephistopheles*, *The Piccadilly Puzzle*, and *The Girl from Malta*, among the others. At the end of the 19$^{th}$ century and during the early 20$^{th}$ century, Hume wrote more than 100 novels, a goodly number of which were mysteries, his most famous being *The Mystery of a Hansom Cab* published in 1886. Recently, the only crime novel I've read is Peter Heller's *The Guide*. Although Heller snapped along quickly through tension, malfeasance, a splattering of blood, and some leavening love, *The Guide* was a nature book as well as a "thriller." Heller knows the outdoors and how to do things, fishing being the primary example in the novel, and the story celebrated seeing and appreciating the natural word while solving a mystery. "Jack [the hero] loved mornings like this," a paragraph began. "The clouds sailed together and multiplied, so that by late morning the sky was a running scud of overcast. The air over the river seemed relieved of relentless sun and released a wealth of summer smells—the damp of exposed roots, the fair sweetness of black-eyed Susans, a watery scent of crushed horsetails. And rain. The promise of it."

"The farm is a nursery of miracles," Poultney Bigelow wrote. While reading *The Guide*, I began rereading Edwin Way Teale's *A Naturalist Buys an Old Farm*. The volume is the best of Teale's books. In it he described living on 130 acres of what once was a small farm in Hampton, Connecticut. He wandered wood and field, observed animals and plants, and mulled lives, those of people and those of the nonhuman. He watched beavers in the moonlight and described the amblings of skunks and opossums who, alas, don't remember that we were once friends. He quoted an elderly neighbor who said that when she was a girl, "what we now call wildlife we just called life." While most travel books celebrate movement, nature writing usually illustrates the pleasures of being stationary. Birchmore rode a bicycle around the world. Teale and his wife stayed on the farm. In comparison to Birchmore, they appear reclusive. But they are not. A companionable world surrounded them. I have read nature writing since childhood and will do so as long as possible after I drift pass eighty headed for one hundred and twenty.

After finishing travel books, I send them back on their journeys and donate them to the Mansfield Library's yearly sale. The only exceptions are Richard Halliburton's books in which I scrawled my name as a child, usually "Sammy Pickering" but sometimes "Sammie" and once "Doll Baby Lamb," an affectionate term Mother applied to me. On my bookshelves is a small library of natural history books. Fifty or sixty are field guides. A few authors are British, among them, "essential" writers like Gilbert White and Richard Jefferies. However, most of the authors are Americans. They wrote primarily about New England and the bordering mid-Atlantic states and preached seeing and appreciating the immediate, among others, John Burroughs, Charles Conrad Abbott, William Hamilton Gibson. In part they appeal to me because they wrote in and about the nineteenth century. Rarely was their prose breathless, and reading them allowed me to breathe deeply, look out my study window, and see the immediate: a goldfinch on the birdbath, a robin with its orange breast buffed and ripe as the sunset.

I own several copies of *Walden Pond*, all paperbacks and marked, the covers flimsy and slick, not like the musty old boards binding Abbott and Gibson, and me. Years ago I wrote an introduction to an edition of *Walden*. For me Thoreau is a source of quotations. Despite his many memorable suggestions, he is not a guide to the impossible life I imagine living apart from the everyday bustle and rancor of pills, flat tires, and telephone solicitations. In the "Spring" chapter of *Walden* Thoreau observes the various geological formations exposed by a cut made for a railroad. He wonders what Champollion [ student of hieroglyphics] "will decipher this hieroglyphic for us." Instead of digging deep and interpreting, I want to notice scoliid wasps and seven son tree, its blossoms fragrant as jasmine and shaking with bumblebees. I want to recognize trident and paperbark maples and along stone walls surrounding old pastures smell apples and black walnuts. I want to amble the yard and woods behind my house and see coral fungus, violet cort its caps in party dress purple and white, and old man of the woods, the dark gray cap of this last prickly and looking unshaven. In August I brought home a giant puffball that the university grounds crew had tossed on a truck to be dumped into a landfill along with webs of broken limbs. I walked around the yard spanking the puffball and becoming practically invisible amid a cloud of cinnamon spores. "Maybe," I told Vicki, "giant puffballs will join chicken of the woods fruiting like cabbage in the yard.

While polishing his prose and writing seductively about how to live, Thoreau abstained from actual living. He didn't marry and have children. He lived by himself and preached the virtues of simplicity. A person may wish for simplicity, but if he has three children as Vicki and I did, the wish will not become actuality. Love and responsibility complicate, and enrich. "Thank goodness," I think, having lived with, rather than by any "the book." "What we want to see," Robert Louis Stevenson wrote, is a person "who can breast into the world, do a man's work, and still reserve his first and pure enjoyment of existence." The nature I appreciate could be thought wallpaper. It won't hide imbecilic behavior, but that's all right. My observations won't change perception, but maybe a paragraph will encourage someone to stretch a passing glance into awareness. Eighty-year-olds should not attempt to suck the marrow out of life. Who wants to risk swallowing false teeth? But an occasional sip is quite pleasant. How nice to notice the flowering of a Japanese Pagoda tree and see a great egret flying over Mirror Lake its white wings curling like foam. The new Sammy Pickering is nine months old and has begun to crawl. Yesterday Edward sent Vicki and me a video of Sammy's weaving and humping across a rug like a fat tobacco hornworm. "It won't be long before I resume crawling," I wrote Edward this afternoon. "Maybe you could arrange a race between Sammy and me before braconid wasps cripple me."

I read Teale while the skirt of a hurricane brushed through Storrs. The wind jumped in heavy gusts, and branches became waterlogged and pulling free from trunk collars fell to the ground shattering. In the distance a low rumble rose and sank. Lights in the house jittered but did not go out. I opened a window to smell the rain and watched the storm shake the leaves on the hickory outside my study like maracas. Their upper surfaces shed the water and looked glazed while the lower looked like old table mats forgotten on a summer porch. Tonight will be calmer. I'm going to begin *The Amur River*. I look forward to setting off beside Thubron on a Mongolian horse. Page travel can inflame the mind, but unlike peripatetic travel it rarely disrupts the alimentary canal.

I won't leave the house and accordingly will not need to put Cooper's "Improved Lavement Apparatus" on my bedside table. One hundred and seventy years ago Cooper recommended his apparatus because being "entirely composed of metal without valves" it "cannot become out of order." "The administration of the whole of the fluid, by one stroke of the Piston," Cooper emphasized, avoided the labor of pumping, and prevented "Admission of air into the Bowels." For sensitive travelers desirous of keeping eccoprotic matters private, the apparatus came in a mahogany box. Moreover, to thwart the rude and the curious, the honey chest was equipped with a lock and key. Moreover, since traveling tires me, I'll sleep well and when I wake, as Vicki says, hammocks won't droop below my eyes. However, I hope a few people whom Thubron meets will be oddly shod. If so, perhaps I can discuss the book and winkle in a pun that has long lingered in my desk. According to a papyrus manuscript when leather shoes were a rarity, people strapped dried flat fish to the underside of their feet, eventually giving rise to calling shoe bottoms soles. My friend Josh says a person would have to be shameless to jam that pun into a serious essay. But, hellfire, at eighty only jackasses worry about shame.

# Reading at One Hundred and Twenty

Trilogies add avoirdupois to a writer's reputation. I wrote three books describing my family's years in Australia. The trilogy does not have the literary status of, say, the Oedipus Cycle. But for mature readers whose undergraduate years have long disappeared beneath the horizon and for whom deep thoughts are no longer an assignment but a burden, the books are pleasant reading. The slow turning of their pages does not bring to mind "the turbid ebb and flow of human misery," as Matthew Arnold put it imagining the effect of hearing the roar of breaking waves upon Sophocles. My trilogy is therapeutic. Melancholy plagues old age. After giving me an injection this morning, a doctor said, "You are in fair shape now, but what lies ahead for people your age are neuro-degenerative diseases." A dose of my pages relieves the oppressive "eternal note of sadness" that oldsters often hear. The world may sometimes seem a darkling plain, but at other times, especially in armchair moments, it glimmers with joy and laughter and pages rumply with light ameliorating paragraphs.

The Australian trilogy did not add as much heft to my reputation as I hoped. Perhaps my aspirations were too high. I am now writing a second trilogy. On this occasion my approach is modest. Instead of books, the trilogy will be composed of essays. Forty years ago, I wrote "Reading at Forty." Last week I finished "Reading at Eighty," and, as the title of this piece reveals, I have begun "Reading at One Hundred and Twenty." Starting the essay now seems sensible. If I delay beginning too long, the essay might collapse at a dead end or deteriorate into a "neuro" of words more jumbled than a tag sale. According to Australian folklore once the oozlum bird lifts off the ground it flies in concentric circles. The circles become smaller and smaller until finally the oozlum flies up its own backside and disappears. Essayists behave similarly. They beat about the same topics for years until suddenly they vanish in a pucker leaving only a few tail feathers behind

As people age, their worlds shrink. Instead of breasting the air and exploring new landscapes, they become homebodies and behave like the oozlum. For the record some ornithologists call the oozlum the weegy weegy bird. They attribute its circular flight to the fact of its having only one wing, a metaphoric recognition of the physical and mental deterioration of oldsters. As people know, the expression "on a wing and a prayer" refers to the effort to accomplish something that has only a slight chance of success. For birders the phrase does not originate from describing a pilot's attempt to fly a crippled aircraft. Instead birders attribute it to the flight of the weegy weegy, "impossible," as one field guide puts it, "without prayer and the willing suspension of disbelief." Recently people whom I haven't seen for decades have begun to circle their pasts. A fortnight ago a man whom I taught at Princeton in 1969 when I was a preceptor drove to Storrs to see me. Vicki and I ate lunch with him and his wife. Fifty-two years ago my wings were full feathered, and I was a colorful high and low flyer. The lunch was enjoyable, but struggling to appear more than a tottery guy on the cusp of neurodegeneration exhausted me, and afterward I indulged in the old man's great pleasure, an afternoon nap. Two days later I received an email from a member of my eighth-grade class at Parmer School in Nashville in 1955. I hadn't thought about my correspondent since I donned long trousers and entered high school. "Sixty-six years. Next a bassinet companion from your wailing days in the delivery room will write you," Vicki said.

Vicki was prescient. My friend Billy and I were born in Nashville on the same day in 1941. For decades we've sent each other birthday greetings. Until this year all our letters were light-hearted celebrations of the present and the future. This September Billy did not write about the future. He had lost insouciance, and dipping his wings, circled the past. "I sailed through seventy and sixty and all the way back to thirty without much concern," he wrote. "But eighty? It troubles me. I remember our attending Paul's sixty-fifth birthday together. We were also sixty-five. Life seemed less complicated, and I wasn't so anxious. Now Paul is dead, and worry keeps me up at night."

Suddenly my birthday shifted from being the conclusion to the second part of a trilogy to becoming the preface to a third. The cards I received were ordinary. Only a few bubbled, but none were flat or bit like vinegar. Vicki's was the brightest and headiest. A field of sunflowers stretched open-faced across the front of her card. "May all your tomorrows be filled with sunflowers," she wrote. "So much," I thought, for old age's being "the Unadorned Years," as one card labeled it. "Hear Ye! Hear Ye!," a bell ringer announced on the cover of another card. Inside he declared "Thou art olde!" Maybe, I thought, I'll endure long enough to be one of those sinners "cotched out" so late, as the gospel song phrases it, that I won't find the "latch to the golden gate." Then I'll skip to the end of the trilogy, maybe even jog on to an afterword entitled "Reading at One Hundred and Sixty or Brave New 2101."

Holmgren Subaru said, "we love having you part of our Subaru family" so much so they offered to reduce any purchase I made over two hundred dollars by twenty-five dollars, or if I were feeling less expansive fifteen dollars off purchases ranging from a hundred dollars to one hundred and ninety-nine dollars and ninety-nine cents "From Your Friends at Storrs Family Dentistry," read the salutation at the end of an email, its effect utilitarian reminding me that I was scheduled to have my teeth cleaned in November. My birthday was mentioned on WILI, the radio station in Willimantic, and twice when Vicki and I walked to CVS to fetch prescriptions, people greeted us and sang "Happy Birthday." Among the more tangible delights was a Wine Country Gift Basket purchased by my jogging buddy David. "Happy birthday to you. / You've had quite a few," David wrote. "May you have even more: / At least one or two." The basket overflowed with palatable cheer. Three bottles of Coppola wine, a Merlot, Chardonnay, and a Cabernet Sauvignon, sat in the spillage from a cornucopia of edibles: cranberry and sesame cookies, cracked peppercorn crackers, Hot Honey Crunch, bacon and habanero bits, hummus, apricots, garlic and herb dip seasoning, green and black olives, and artichoke snacks amid sundry others.

Vicki's and my children, Francis, Edward, and Eliza gave me a gift that invigorated the "achy years ahead," as one realistic well-wisher dubbed his and, by extension, my future. On my 70th birthday, the children sent Vicki and me to Provincetown on Cape Cod. This year they surprised us with days in Newport, another place we hadn't visited. They underwrote three nights in the Jailhouse Inn, a celebratory meal at the Castle Hill Inn, and purchased membership for us in the Preservation Society of Newport County to insure that we would visit the famous gilded mansions. "Don't," I told them on our return from Rhode Island "plan a trip for my 90th birthday, at least not quite yet."

Newport is only two hours from Storrs. But in the prospect short trips to the immediate now appear more arduous to me than long trips to the far. For both journeys dogs must be boarded and bags packed. But in the case of the nearby one doesn't hop on an airplane and leave the driving to someone else. As a person ages, not only does reading become repetitious but he also limits travel to the comfortably familiar, in Vicki's and my case, cruises in the Caribbean. Anxiety tarnishes the prospect of the new while memory burnishes the old and makes the oft-repeated appear easy. Pills and fretfulness are the companions of age. "I wish the kids had given me a chocolate cake," I said to Vicki before we left Connecticut. "I'm bound to get lost going to Newport. The car will break down. Then what?" "Just set the GPS and follow her instructions," Vicki said. I did, and in retrospect the drive was simple, although at least half a dozen times I shouted, "Oh, lord, Vicki, which exit should I take?" The trip home was a different matter. We didn't get lost, but the GPS steered us through a tangle of secondary roads in rural Connecticut. Some were so rough and pocked they looked like beaches on which leatherhead turtles had dug nests for their eggs. Even worse halfway to Storrs, a yellow light on the instrument panel snapped on warning that a tire was low. On the remainder of the drive my nerves frayed more than the tire. Still we reached Langdon Tire in Willimantic without sinking to a rim, and a mechanic repaired the tire.

The Jailhouse Inn was on Marlborough Street near the harbor and the center of old Newport. From there Vicki and I roamed along America's Cup Avenue and explored the shopping wharfs. The area was familiar reminding me of streets near cruise ship docks in the Caribbean. Shopkeepers didn't hawk jewelry with the hard-sell familiarity that merchants in the Caribbean hustled diamonds, but they were aggressive. Before leaving the hotel Vicki slung an old carryall from a Holland America trip over her shoulder. "Off the ship," a man said noticing the name of the cruise line on the bag and striding up to us. "I've got just the things for you. They will make your vacation. Come inside."

For four dollars we rode the bus trolley around the town. We roamed Thames and Spring Street, Broadway and Washington Square. While we walked the first afternoon, a thunderstorm broke low over our heads like a hammer hitting an anvil and throwing sparks. To escape the rain and lightning we darted into Pour Judgement, a pinched hall-like one-room bar on Broadway. Along one side of the hall ran a tight row of small tables, on the other, the bar itself. The bar was elbow to elbow, nose to nose with people. Only employees wore masks. Even if Columbus enlisted the aid of a miscellany of explorers—Magellan, Captain Cook, and Marco Polo—he could not have discovered any more masks in Newport. Waitresses wore black sweatshirts. Printed on the backs in white letters was "Last Night I Used

Pour Judgment." Vicki and I were cold and tired, so we ordered large glasses of Pour Judgment pilsner. We also ordered bowls of Guatemalan Seafood Soup and divided a BLT. On trips happenstance is often so unpleasant that it colors memory. Of course, over time the memories become the stuff of fond anecdotes. In contrast Pour Judgment was memorable because the food was so good, I almost bought a sweatshirt. A spiced shellfish-tomato broth thick with a reef of diced vegetables, shrimp, salmon, and cod, the soup was better than any seafood gumbo I'd eaten in New Orleans. Although people don't usually travel to eat, food invariably seasons journeys, in my case frequently causing gastric weather systems tumultuous with wind and rain, cold and heat. In Newport, we dined high and low, and well.

Soup at Pour Judgment was twelve dollars a bowl. Dinner at Castle Hill cost much more. I am not stingy, but I am ill at ease with compliments, be they verbal or financial. I don't know whether that reflects age or surfeit. I'd rather people spend on themselves what they consider spending on me. That caveat aside, the set three-course dinner at Castle Hill was ninety-two dollars. A sampler of three wines cost between thirty-six or forty-five dollars. "You should have aged beyond monetary concern. Enjoy the evening and this token of the children's affection," Vicki said. I did. The drive down Bellevue and along Ocean Drive beside the coast was soothing. Few cars were on the road, and as it set, the sun mellowed, and the glare vanished. At the Inn Vicki and I sat in a nook looking out over Narragansett Bay and watched orange and pink sink below the horizon and the sky turn dark blue then black and velvety. Eating in the inn delighted me in part because it was once the summerhouse of Alexandre Agassiz, the son of Louis Agassiz, the Harvard zoologist and geologist, a man whose presence I've stumbled upon in the course of my ecological meanderings. Alexandre himself was a prominent marine biologist. Although the Castle Inn in which we ate was nothing like the summerhouse built in 1874, I liked imagining that the pages I wrote about wood and field were part of a natural history continuum. Intensifying the feeling were both the dim light that allowed me to dream and the formal and personal presentation of the meal which made me feel if not special, at least momentarily chosen—a dangerous feeling on days other than a birthday.

The meal was fine, but it was almost incidental to our enjoyment. For an appetizer I had rabbit galantine, a dish of which I'd never heard and the taste of which I didn't know how to appreciate. For the main course I ate sea bass and Vicki halibut. For dessert Vicki had hazelnut chocolate cake, and I, a chocolate log covered with a red wine sauce, a candle sticking out of the middle and accompanied by our hostess's singing 'Happy Birthday." The evening accomplished its purpose. As could be expected, the prospect of driving back to mid-town in the dark worried me, but we left the inn feeling affectionate and proud of our achievement: our three thoughtful children. "Age intensifies the weakness for criticism, but for the next forty years you shouldn't complain about anything that has to do with family," Vicki said.

The Jailhouse Inn was built at the end of the 18th century. Until 1986, it housed the Newport Police Department. With twenty-three rooms and a parking space allotted to each room, the inn was small. The rooms themselves were modest and irregularly shaped, cell-like, but alive in contrast, say, to the pastel anonymity of a Marriott or Comfort Inn. On the walls hung pictures of policemen, and suspended along corridors were heavy old cell doors. Greeting us when we arrived in our room were presents from the children, wine and a wooden box containing artisanal chocolates. Food always seemed on the table, in our room or out. Every morning a buffet breakfast was set out in the dining room, and tea, coffee, and homemade cookies were available throughout the day.

After breakfast each morning we drove to the three great Gilded-Age houses open and managed by the Preservation Society: The Breakers, Marble House, and The Elms. Built as a summerhouse for the Vanderbilt family and completed in 1893, The Breakers consisted of 138,300 square feet. The Italianate rooms were so mesmerizingly beautiful and ornate they eventually seemed ugly. After a while their expensive contents devolved into clutter and smacked of the grotesque antiques and statuary sold on Fort Lauderdale's Las Olas Boulevard by stores pandering to the poor taste of wealthy riffraff. The decorations and great rooms never awakened envy. Instead I came to think the house a prison. I pitied the pampered inhabitants who could not, I imagined, escape the cells of birth and the defects caused by wealth. As I studied the rooms, I thought of Thoreau. "How many a poor immortal soul have I met well-nigh crushed and smothered under its load, creeping down the road of life," he wrote, "pushing before it a barn seventy-five feet by forty, its Augean stables never cleansed, and one hundred acres of land, tillage, mowing, pasture and wood-lot!" The library was not a reading room but a place which distracted from reading, the walnut paneling with its acanthus vines and urns and the coffered ceiling awash with dolphins drawing eyes from the page and promoting sleep rather than thought. Within many people, certainly me, lurks an imp or perhaps more seriously a sans-culotte. As I stood in the library, I imagined scattering a handful of busty Harlequin romances or the three volumes of Faulkner's Snopes trilogy on the tables. I wondered how long Erskine Caldwell's *Tobacco Road* and *God's Little Acre* would last on the shelves. "A long time if they were leather-bound," Vicki said.

Only the entombed are consistent. The Breakers so attracted and repulsed me that if Vicki and I go back to Newport we'll spend another day there. After I left the house, what clung to my mind? Oddly, but I suppose in character, I remembered a portrait along the foreground of which inched a turtle. The day after Vicki and I returned to Storrs, we walked the floodplain on Spring Valley Farm. The colors of fall reminded me of the dining room in Marble House. Sassafras glowed orange and pink. The leaves of staghorn sumac smoldered red and burnt while those on grape vines were majolica-ed, yellow and brown, spotted and holed. No turtle crawled through the grass on the plain, but we saw a host of small creepers and crawlers: fall field crickets, praying mantises, Carolina and marsh meadow grasshoppers, a masked shrew, and the year's last dragonflies, autumn meadow hawks, one of which perched on my shoulder and hitched a ride across a dirt road.

My favorite house was The Elms. When we toured it, I was tired. As a result it seemed less fussy than either The Breakers or Marble House. Moreover, the lawn behind the house spread flat and manicured inviting appreciation. The namesake trees, elms, had died and been replaced by beeches, European, European Weeping, and the occasional Fern Leaf beech. The trees were massive, and their limbs dangled in loose struts and humped across the ground forming great umbrellas. Knobs protruded like eyeballs from trunks where limbs had snapped off. Crowds had carved their initials into the trunks, but Time muddied their letters as it does lives themselves, both those of the carvers and those of the owners of the house.

Inside the house my eyes rolled dizzily, the plethora of ornamentation graying sight like glaucoma. Outside, the broad comparatively empty lawn enabled sight to rest, allowing me to notice likeable things, beside the back terrace, two sculptures, the first of a lion heavy atop the belly of a dying crocodile, the reptile's mouth open, its teeth filed but useless, the second of a lioness holding food for her two cubs in her mouth, a large bird, a circlet of feathers atop its head, probably an East African Crowned Crane, its neck slack as rope. I strolled down the lawn to a modest alley of cedar trees. They brought to mind my grandfather's farm in Virginia where a lane of red cedars flowed down a slope to a thicket of bamboo. At night my friends and I hid amid the trees and pretending we were bears jumped out at each other growling. We didn't hide in the bamboo because we believed copperheads slid through them prowling the night.

At The Elms on a terrace above the cedar trees stood a fountain. The fountain was hideous, but I noticed it because it was "creaturely." Four cupbearers supported a scallop shell. Around the lip of the shell turtles sunned themselves while water sprayed from their mouths. "They are everyday painted turtles," I told Vicki. "How do you know?" Vicki asked. "I know such things," I answered. "Study the lawn, and you'll see a few dandelions. They are homey and domestic, our flowers." Noticing the turtles and the dandelions pleased me. I suppose I was colonizing a small part of The Elms. That's what readers and writers and birthday celebrants do.

Walking begets walking, and good feelings. After leaving The Elms we did the greater part of the cliff walk along Easton Bay, doubling back and forth from the North End pass the Forty Steps, Salve Regina University, and The Breakers to Ochre Point. At the Point we stopped because the trail shattered into rubble. Once I could have hop-scotched forward, but I was no longer limber, and the slight tilts and the up-and-down looseness of the stones dissuaded me. We ambled three and a half miles. The trail was easy, suitable for children and "tourists international," that is, house hunters whose ownership is limited to viewing. The cliff was modest, not like the jagged trenched bluffs at Cape St. Mary's, close to Four Winds, our place in Nova Scotia. On the passable portion of the trail, walkers did not have to mind their steps, and they talked about the houses they visited and speculated about their owners. "How rich were the Vanderbilts?" a woman asked her husband. "I don't know, but they sure as Hell weren't Communists," the man answered. Near Ochre Point an osprey perched on a lip of granite, always a treat to see, but for the most part the walk was barren, all wildlife, we decided, swept offshore by climate change and by pesticides, the greening chemicals sprayed on the grand lawns of Marble House and The Elms. Still we enjoyed strolling, and before returning to our car Vicki bounced down the steep Forty Steps like a teenager.

During the holiday after exploring the tourist

downtown, we sought respite in Trinity Church. The church sat atop a slight hill above Queen Anne Square and Thames Street. During the day the hillside was still and trim; at night it was weedy with assignations. Although the church had undergone many changes, it was mortared to the past and in one form or another was three hundred years old. Like many other churches, Trinity was modeled on the Georgian designs of Christopher Wren and shared a muted gray elegance with St. George's Episcopal Church in Nashville which I attended as a child. St. George's lacked a tiered wineglass pulpit, boxed pews, and Trinity's long history, but it was similarly mannered and was a haven apart from worldly fret. Unlike the interiors of the gilded houses which caffeinated, the nave of Trinity invited a person to sit quietly and iron wrinkles out of thought and mood. Memorials lined the walls of the nave. They offered glimpses into lives and evoked almost sensory flavors of the past. In a sense they were historical graffiti. Unlike contemporary scribblings which blare across the sides of buildings, railway cars, and beams of highway bridges, sometimes it seems everywhere, plaques in the church did not soil sight. Instead, while the memorials made viewers aware of human frailty and man's capacity for violence, they also framed lives in ways that did not exclude the possibility of order and elegance. My favorite memorial was that of Georgina Clarke Pell who died in London in 1851. "She was," her tablet declared, "of a particular beauty, tender and dutiful of heart to God and man, and breathing through all her loveliness a charm of innocent unconsciousness."

Although trips tire, they also awaken. After arriving home I started reading George Barr McCutcheon's novels. McCutcheon wrote during the

Gilded Age and into the Twenties. I began with one of his more popular novels, *Graustark The Story Of A Love Behind A Throne*. It was published 120 years ago in 1901 and added a spurious but odd synchronicity to "Reading at One Hundred and Twenty." For the oozlum-like essayist page-worthy things happen one after another. Sometimes they are related; often they are not. Shortly after Vicki and I returned home, Eliza telephoned. Although Eliza had a license, she hadn't driven a car since she entered college eighteen years ago. She told us she was taking refresher lessons so she could manage highways in California. The first lesson lasted two hours. "My instructor," she said, "never stopped talking about former students who'd been killed in crashes." "How many?" I asked. "Probably eight or nine," she said. "I was too nervous to keep track."

The next morning Vicki and I had coffee at Dog Lane Café. A student and her father sat at a table next to us, and I overheard their conversation. Their talk would have startled courtiers in Graustark. "Dad," the student said, her voice rising in frustration, "I have been taking the pill since 2018." As much as the overheard lends itself to paragraphs, in this instance I would have preferred silence and thinking about Graustark's fanciful gold throne "inlaid with precious stones—diamonds, rubies, emeralds, sapphires and other wondrous jewels." The inhibited courtships of McCutcheon's novels appeal to me more than the pharmacology of contemporary mating. At the end of *Graustark*, the hero and heroine walked along a balcony, moonlight pouring over them like music. They said little. "Love obstructs the flow of speech; the heartbeats choke back the words and fill the throat," McCutcheon wrote. "Times there were when they covered the full length of the balcony without a word. And yet they understood each other. The mystic, the enchanting silence of love was fraught with a conversation felt, not heard." "That's not material raw enough for Netflix or Hulu," Vicki said. "Today's popular love scene requires either a pistol or some raucous animal grunting."

Lives often seem miscellanies or, perhaps, anthologies of the unrelated—here a limerick, there a riddle, on the desk a short story, and neglected under an armchair a novel and a memoir. Reading is similar. When looked at through the perspective of a life or of forty years, reading that initially appeared fragmentary seems part of a whole. Four days after returning from Newport, I stuffed maps and notes into a folder at the back of a drawer in my desk. "That ends that," I told Vicki. "A good time, but by Friday Newport will have slipped from mind." Two days later we received an email from the Preservation Society. In less than a month, the email announced, holidays would begin at the Newport Mansions. In the Society's greenhouses, "more than 500 poinsettias, started from cuttings, have been growing since mid-April." In August 1200 Oriental lilies sprouted from bulbs. "Now they are reaching maturity, just in time to be placed in The Breakers, Marble House, and The Elms as part of the extensive decorations. We hope you will visit." "We will," Vicki declared, "if not this December certainly some Christmas before you write "Reading at One Hundred and Sixty."

As eighty disappeared amid the broken signatures of the past, I wondered what would curtail my reading—health, the demands of caring for the house and Vicki, and, of course, worry about unrecognized matters that did not concern me a decade ago. Because

I will be physically and mentally less vigorous, perhaps I'll read more. Still, no longer do I read two books at a sitting. The day when I'll make it through only a hundred pages may be approaching, but perhaps those pages will be weightier than the stacks of yellow-backed dime novels I once binged on like a birthday boy shoveling down chocolate cake. Recently my days had not belonged to books. A person cannot predict what life will toss his way. On Wednesday, Vicki and I drove across the state to Farmington for our annual appointment with a dermatologist. On our return three miles from Storrs something bounced up from the road ahead of us and slammed into the front of the car. The object wasn't big, "about the size of a rubber doorstop," I told Vicki. Because it did not affect driving, we forgot about it. The next day the car stayed in the garage until evening when we decided to take advantage of a two-for-the-price-of-one deal at Blaze Pizza. The trip downtown was normal, but as we headed back, the dashboard erupted in a frenzy of red and yellow urging me to "Check Engine" and issuing a mysterious warning labeled "Eye Sight." Suddenly a small gray car resembling a Christmas ornament began trundling back and forth across the odometer.

Nowadays I think almost as much when asleep as when awake. In the middle of the night, it "dawned" on me that the object that bounced into our car knocked out the lane changing camera and jump-started the small car on the dashboard. I got out of bed early and backed the car out of the garage. The grill was snaggle-toothed. At 8:30 I was on the road to Holmgren Subaru fifteen miles away in North Franklin. While the driving was smooth, my nerves were bumpy. I imagined the car erupting in a ball of flame or in more reasonable moments dying and in its last gasp wheeling into its own grave in a ditch deep beside the road. "Lordy," I mumbled. "I can't buy a new car." In the three years I'd owned the Subaru, I'd mastered few of the car's helpful, time-saving devices. In fact, opening the hood before I left Storrs took twenty minutes of hide-and-seek, rather find-the-mysterious-levers, the game punctuated by a manual of untoward language. On a new car, useful devices were certain to be more reclusive and complex and thus sources of angina, not heart ease.

Shortly after beginning to work on my car, a mechanic came into the waiting room. He held a cell phone. "This is what shattered the grill and caused the trouble," he said. "I found it on the bumper behind the grill." While opening the door to put groceries onto, say, the back seat, someone must have laid his phone atop his car. He forgot about it, and later the phone blew off the roof and whipped into the front of my car. Forgetting items on the roofs of cars is common. Usually, the objects are handbags. In past years I found four purses in the middle of roads. One contained six hundred and fifty dollars. I always located the owners although it sometimes took two days. Repairs and a new grill cost me more than seven hundred dollars. "That's a lot of money. Did you try to contact the owner of the phone?" Vicki asked later. "No," I said. "The phone was locked, and its innards probably shattered. Such things happen and stewing about the expense causes discontent." "If your phone had damaged a stranger's car, would you have paid for the repairs?" Vicki asked. "Of course," I said. "Well, then," Vicki started. "There will be nothing beyond 'well then,'" I interrupted, shutting off the conversation.

To fill the hours while my car was being repaired,

I carried *Beverly of Graustark*, another of McCutcheon's novels with me to Holmgren. Beverly was an old-fashioned peach. "Miss Beverly was neither tall nor short," McCutcheon wrote. "She was of that divine and indefinite height known as medium; slender but perfectly molded; strong but graceful, an absolutely healthy young person whose beauty knew well how to take care of itself. Being quite heart-whole and fancy-free, she slept well, ate well, and enjoyed every minute of life." In *King Lear* ripeness was all. In romantic narratives delayed anticipation is a pleasure. Before biting into an account of the flirtatious doings of the luscious maiden, I met other characters. Sounding more like a writer than a nobleman, a prince said, "I am the native of the vast domain known to a few of us as Circumstance." Although the prince dressed like a goat herder, readers of love stories immediately saw through the disguise and knew he was Beverly's husband-to-be.

Mechanical circumstances filled the waiting room at Holmgren with people, and their conversation distracted me from reading. One man had two daughters. The elder was forty and had two children; the younger was thirty-three and had twelve. "I like them," he said, "but I've only got four fishing rods." Near the end of his second tour in Vietnam, another man was shot. "Thank goodness," he said, "else I might have stayed in the army." "Before my heart attack," a third man said, "I was a great hunter. Inside my barn I mounted the antlers of more than twenty deer. Over the door are the heads of an albino and a black deer." "I no longer hunt," a fourth man said. "I don't miss it. What I really miss is reloading shells. Whenever I became nervous, I'd go to the basement and reload shells. That always calmed me down."

Conversation in the waiting room was prelude to a circus. At noon three dogs and their owners strolled in. Ruby was a furry adolescent labradoodle; D'Artagnan, a harlequin Great Dane, and Harley, a low-slung hound and pit bull mix, his muzzle long and narrow like that of a dachshund, not bullish and trap-like. The dogs had come for a "Subaru Loves Pets Event." The usual Ascents and Foresters had been moved to one end of the showroom to make room for an obstacle course consisting of fences, hurdles, and a tunnel, among other devices to challenge the abilities of "muttatheletes." Salesmen wore orange Subaru Loves Pets tee-shirts. Posters in the room announced that Subaru would donate one hundred dollars to Wings of Freedom for "every shelter pet adopted in October." Of particular concern were Underdogs, animals "with special needs like the older, deaf, blind and 'different.'" Displayed throughout the room were treats. I gathered a selection for our underdogs, a bag of Snausages, Pigs in a Blanket baked for canine tastes, and a five-inch bone covered with sprinkles. For Vicki I brought home a pink dog bandana decorated with white dog footprints, the name Subaru, and the company's starry logo. I also picked up an orange Frisby and an orange capsule which could be packed with poop bags and fastened on a leash. The jewel of my foraging was a "Chewbaru Outbark," a stuffed cloth-covered chewy squeaky toy, a model Outback, nine and a half inches long, four and a half broad, and four tall from the bottom of its wheels to the rack on the roof.

Our underdogs liked the Snausages, and as a present for Beatrice, an Old English Bulldog belonging to Erica, Edward's wife, Vicki packed the Chewbaru Outbark in a box she mailed to South Carolina. Before falling asleep, I read more of *Beverly*. Fancy appeals to one hundred- and twenty-year-old readers more than realism. McCutcheon's heroes and heroines stumbled star-crossed through chapters of swampy purple prose along the way being bushwhacked by devious rivals and demonic villains. However, at the conclusion of their ordeals true love won the day and cleared the night. I have long enjoyed impossible happy endings, more so now as the ending ahead is simply an ending. Like Truxton King, the hero of the novel by the same name and next book by McCutcheon I read, I "believed in Romance" when I was young. Like King, I also "believed in Santa Claus and the fairies" and "grew up with an ever-increasing bump of imagination," in my case a large occipital bun which Mother called "a stingy bump."

Graustark and one of the favorite imaginary nations of my childhood Anthony Hope's Ruritania shared a narrative border and many of the same active verbs. For a signature of pages, I accompanied Truxton to Edelweiss, but then I absented myself from swashbuckling to drive Vicki to an eye doctor in West Hartford. Sometimes I fear that I'll be studying stone tablets not pages at one hundred and twenty and that the volume of my doings may close before I complete the reading trilogy. Time and grinding appointments never stop paring my energy. Driving to West Hartford was a nerve-buckling adventure. Blackout curtains of rain swept across the windshield. Wind galloped and reared. The highway disappeared into fog banks, and other cars became invisible enveloped in sprays of their making. Eventually I left the interstate and traveled on side roads to avoid traffic jams. Although roads were clearer, they were not cleaner. Fall is the great harvesting season of animals, and the shoulders of the roads looked like sinks soiled with dishrags.

After Vicki's examination, the rain stopped momentarily, and I drove to Trader Joe's to purchase treats for our friend David. Driving exhausted me, and I decided to remain in the car while Vicki shopped, but then a pickup truck backed into the parking space in front of me. Pasted on the tail gate were two stickers. One read "F**K Biden," the other "Gun Control Means Using Two Hands." "Not the reading of any decent human being," I muttered and went into the store. The manager greeted me. "Can I help you?" she asked. "No," I said, "I'm just wet and cold and tired." "Wait here," she said and walked over to a counter. She returned with a packet of Trader Joe's "Dark Chocolate Covered Almonds." "Take two of these now and two more when you leave the store. They will put you back on your feet," she said, handing me the packet. I followed her instructions. When I left for Storrs, I didn't notice if the pickup was still in the lot. The candy was so tasty I overdosed, but what made me really feel good was the woman's generous nature. Waiting at home was another spirit raiser, pictures of Sammy taken in the daycare he attends three days a week. One was a study in white and brown of Sammy and Alianna, both ten months old. In the picture the two children stood on opposite sides of a low table and leaning across held hands. Parked behind them on the table was a green dump truck. In Alianna's hair was a white bow, around Sammy's neck, a red bandana. I imagined Sammy and Alianna's friendship thriving in a kinder world.

Sadly, people may change but not human nature. Nevertheless, when I resumed reading *Truxton King* I felt refreshed. A portrait of King by Harrison Fisher appeared on the cover of the book. Fisher painted more than three hundred covers for *Cosmopolitan*, and his "Fisher Girl" was as famous at "The Gibson Girl." King was clearly related to the girls. He was slim-wasted, and his legs, long and thin. He wore brown half chaps with buckles, jodhpur boots, and flared-hipped riding breeches. His feet were narrow and looked incapable of supporting the weight of excitement. He wore a long-sleeved shirt with its sleeves rolled neatly up above the elbow exposing forearms so smooth they seemed manicured. To light a cigarette, he cupped his hands before his face. He looked like a pleasantly boring tablemate at a dinner party, not a twenty-six-year-old monied adventurer who roamed all the desolate places depicted in a child's atlas, a man whose dallying in revolutions led to a price being put on his head in South America.

On the page he was a different man, "tall, raw-boned, rangy" with "a face so tanned by wind and sun you had the impression that his skin would feel like leather if you could affect the impertinence to test it by the sense of touch." He'd spent the "full allotted" time in college where he hadn't escaped "the usual number of 'conditions' that dismay but do not discourage the happy-go-lucky undergraduate who makes two or three teams with comparative ease, but who has a great deal of difficulty with physics or whatever else he actually is supposed to acquire between the close of the football season and the opening of base-ball practice." Like me he'd read a great number of "improbable romances," and we traveled together to Graustark, I, for bedtime entertainment, he, seeking love and excitement. A disciple of Wilkins Micawber, he believed that something was bound to "turn up" in Edelweiss, much as readers and writers hope, nay, expect things will turn up. He said Youth died "when curiosity ends." The same is true of pages. Paragraphs trail into ellipses when curiosity flags. The novel was a carnival of acts and performers: communists, anarchists, muscular illiterate rogues, elegant ladies, melodramatic treachery, castles, underground dungeons, heroic Americans, corseted manners, Dukes, gossamer loves, Duchesses, cannonading, witchery, and a beautiful, misguided bomb thrower whom circumstance and a weak arm reduced to "a quivering, shattered thing." The turmoil exhausted me and at midnight made me hanker for a simple romance, perhaps one from my first forty years of reading, this under palm trees and within hearing of the temple bells of the Moulmein Pagoda.

Banished from Graustark, Count Marlanx was the book's villain. Refusing to accept any punishment and plotting to overthrow Prince Robin the young ruler of Graustark, he resembled Milton's Satan, never admitting that a field or a devious plan was lost. "All is not lost," he seemed to say, "the unconquerable Will, / And study of revenge, immortal hate, / And courage never to submit or yield: / And what is else not to be overcome?" My friend Josh believes that the healthy mind is empty. While a full mind reduces flexibility, emptiness invigorates and almost invites curiosity. An excess of memories clogs, "something particularly true," he thinks, "among the aged." Like all opinionated people, Josh is right and wrong. In addition to Marlanx, several characters in the novel were familiar, recognition of which made reading more enjoyable, particularly for former teachers. Truxton was a lively affectionate Tom Jones, his libido controlled by Victorian stays. Prince Robin was a first cousin both of Little Lord Fauntleroy and of the boy in a portrait hanging on the wall of my dining room. That boy's family thought him a Prince and dressed him in a one-piece pink double breasted play suit with white ruffles around the neck and at the end of the sleeves. Both princes were destined to be "good sorts," the phrase happily trite and applicable both to a boy who spent his childhood in Tennessee in the 1940s and to the spirit of Graustark which after the hullabaloos subsided was sappy, more All-American than Central European. Indeed, while Robin's mother was a Princess and a native Graustarkian, his father was another adventuresome American, a hearty Cambridge man, a Dink Stover who not finding the crowd at Yale "corking" hopped a train to Harvard Yard.

*The Prince of Graustark* was published in 1914 five years after *Truxton King*. During the time Prince Robin idled on a narrative siding, fifteen book years passed. On reappearing, Robin was twenty-two years old and traveling across the United States ostensibly to sell bonds to cure Graustark's financial woes, but actually in search of adventure. At the start of the book, he visited Truxton King and an aunt at Red Roof her summer cottage in the Catskills. Close by was one of the homes of William Blithers, perhaps the richest man in the world. Bullheaded, at times coarse, but nonetheless likeable, Blithers was an American go-get-him. Aware of the tradition of cash-short European aristocrats coming to America to marry money, he decided that his daughter Maud should marry Prince Robin, no matter the wishes of either youth. Therein began a goldendoodle tale—a Hallmark romance mixed with the stagecraft of genial slapstick: costume and identity changes, a mysterious woman named B. Guile, screens and doors, mirrors, confusion, conversations overheard and misheard, a shipboard dalliance, hushed sightings in Paris at the Ritz, a police chase with constables on bicycles, and a happy, youth-must-be-served ending. Amid the good cheer of the conclusion, several neglected how's of the plot were forgotten, matters of no consequence to readers beyond a certain age and who long for the lost and impossible truths of fancy.

In J. B. Priestley's *Daylight on Saturday*, Ben Elrick, a superintendent in a wartime airplane plant, addressed both fictional workers on the factory floor and Priestley's sedentary readers. Elrick lamented that society suppressed individuality, thwarted genius and inspiration and forcing people to live mechanically rewarded mindless acquiescence. The war simply exacerbated the pressure to conform. Elrick said a "fire" burned in all people. "Instead of blowing that fire inside us into a blaze we try to damp it down, we try to make the best of what we've got instead of turning what we've got into the best we can imagine." "How else can a decent person burdened with duty and responsibility, with family, behave?" Josh said after I read him the passage. What literate people often do, Josh continued, is read bedtime soporifics, swashbuckling novels chaotic with revolution, better times a-coming, and lives and loves impossible outside the imagination. "Such readers live safely and comfortably, something especially important to people nearing one hundred and twenty strapped to routine by grappling hooks sharp with doctors' appointments and pills, the names of which sound like cities beyond the Caucasus: Metoprolol, Taldykorgan, Akyrtobe, Losartin, and Merki. Although embers from fires like those Elrick envisioned set dry social tinder and tender hearts aflame, things are always damped down and come 'right' at the end." "Perhaps," I thought, "but Josh takes reading too seriously. One of the characteristics of fun in, and out, of books is that it's forgettable."

As a reader clacks over sleepers on his way to one hundred and twenty, incidentals become noticeable, details often peripheral to plots but which remind people of the lives they actually led. Blithers owned a house in Newport, from which he journeyed by private train. He had means beyond the comprehension of the Oelrichs, Berwinds, or Vanderbilts In comparison to his home, The Breakers was a mansionette. I hope some antiquarian writes the Preservation Society, citing *The Prince of Graustark* and asking what happened to the Blithers Estate, its great hall and English dining rooms, the columns of Carrara marble in and without the house, and, of course, the portraits on the walls, especially the one of the former prince from Tennessee. I suspect that as he grew older his blond hair turned brown and that only on special occasions did he wear a suit that glowed "like wine in a sunset."

Bookish fragments deceive older readers into thinking their days are green, even in autumn when their lives are withering. Three weeks ago, Vicki announced that she had confiscated my bicycle, not my car keys, but my bicycle. Yesterday she told me this was the last year I was allowed to blow leaves. "You are too wobbly." Thursday, I cleaned out my locker in the basement of the university gymnasium. I had it for twenty years, and friends decorated the door with found objects. They attached scrunchies, paper clips, soda pop caps, and so many hair pins that the door looked like the tail of a porcupine. Near the top of the door was a small metal sign. Printed on it was "Gabby," a reference to my penchant for anecdotes.

From the locker I removed a tube of sunscreen, plastic containers for water and shampoo, a bar of soap, gloves which I wore outside on cold mornings, and a lap counter I slipped on the index finger of my right hand when I ran inside. I left the door open for the next occupant. Joe who had it before me also used it for twenty years. The next user was bound to be a stranger. Goodbye, I thought as I left the locker room to Joe's and my forty years. Goodbye to Baki, Tom, Lee, Tony, Dick, and Howard. Goodbye to climbing twenty-two steps to the building's first floor with David making loud claps by slapping our feet down simultaneously.

Goodbye to Les's shoes. I couldn't remember anything particular about them. All I recalled was that David and I frequently discussed them and David wrote a poem "Whatever Happened to Les's Shoes?" I'm not an in-the-closet haberdasher, but I remember the first stanza. "Are they under the bed enjoying a snooze, / Or bustling about wherever they choose?" / Have they ventured to take a Caribbean cruise? / Are they down in New Orleans, singin' the blues?" Being bookish, somewhere near the end of the poem David refers to one of my favorite literary characters, asking, "Are they hot on the trail of Goody Two-Shoes, / While minding their p's and minding their q's?" "In the good old locker room time," I thought, emending the title of the Tin Pan Alley summertime song initially published in 1902, one hundred and twenty years ago.

Disengagement was in the air. Two of our small dogs are eighty in human years. The third is seventy-eight. In the past when children came to the front stoop on Halloween, the dogs raced to the door and leapt up pressing their muzzles and paws against the screen. This year not even a pod of newly hatched dragons stirred them, and they did not leave their beds under the kitchen table. "Oh, dear, how sad," Vicki said glancing at the dogs as she snuffed out the candle inside the pumpkin. "I hoped we'd see more trick or treaters," she continued. "There are no young families in the neighborhood. Those dragons don't live on a nearby street. In twelve months they'll molt, shed their baby wings, and go elsewhere. Next year I'm going to skip Halloween. Would you like a Mounds bar? I bought too much candy." "No, thanks," I said.

The next morning the leaf blower started after only eighteen tries. I have now finished the initial trilogy of blowing, raking, and carting. The chore took thirteen hours, an hour longer than last year. But I accomplished it in three days rather than the usual four. Before fall becomes winter, I'll have cleaned the yard two more times. Today sparkled. The sky was washed and blue, and the sunlight, silver. A freshening, almost frosty wind welled up and swept across the yard. Blue jays shrieked, and Carolina wrens laughed. The dirt smelled bacterial, and I scrubbed a fist of earthworm castings into the lifelines on my palms. Leaves drizzled from sugar maples. Light shimmered through them turning them iridescent and bright yellow. The leaves of red maples slipped less noticeably to the ground. Once there they blossomed, the upper or adaxial surfaces scarlet. the under surfaces pink and sometimes purple. That morning I left the house weary. That afternoon I returned invigorated. All my parts either ached or throbbed, but I felt alive. After I dumped the last leaves in the wood behind the house, I brewed a pot of Yorkshire tea and ate a Mounds bar. "We'll see about next year. Maybe a catacomb of skeletons and a coven of witches will appear," I said to Vicki.

In the eighteenth-century moralists criticized reading novels and romances, arguing that by appealing to the imagination they undermined reason and freed readers from the healthy restraints of conscience. In 1730, a writer in the *Universal Spectator, and Weekly Journal* said that romances ruined "more Virgins than Masquerades or Brothels." "I leave you to judge," the writer warned, "what an excellent Housewife a Damsel is likely to make, who has read the *Persian Tales* and fancies herself a Sultana." Dr. Johnson wrote that "Works of Fiction" were especially dangerous "to the Young, the Ignorant, and the Idle, to whom they serve as Lectures of Conduct, and Introductions into Life." I am a house husband not a housewife. I don't patronize brothels or frequent masquerades. I don't fancy myself a Sultan or a Sultana or, in this time of flexible genderism, an exotic blend of the two. I am neither ignorant nor young, but being retired I am idle especially in evenings.

Novels have not served as introductions to my daylight life of flat tires and leaf blowers. But when reason dozes, novels like the Graustark series influence my life. Not long ago I dreamed a bruiser knocked down Vicki outside the portcullis to a castle. Seizing the man's arm, I reacted like Truxton King and whirling him around like a bolas tossed him into a moat. Water splashed up and soaked me, causing me to wake. By the time I fell back asleep, the brigand had vanished into some mountain fastness "in the hills of Dawsbergen." If he ever appears near the keep again, I'll grab his sword and whack him on the head, or "hair pasture" as a hero with cosmetologist leanings described the cranium of a scoundrel in a novel I read last year.

After I read four Graustark novels, kings and queens lost their glitter, and the exotic staled. The time had come for me to return to America and to know Mr. Thomas Bingle of New York, a prince of a man, a poor bookkeeper dressed in the tattered but royal robes of good deeds, these, alas, shredded by the ridicule and neglect of the worldly. *Mr Bingle* was McCutcheon's version of *A Christmas Carol.* In fact, every Christmas, Bingle read the *Carol* aloud before he and Mrs. Bingle ate dinner. While Bingle himself was McCutcheon's Bob Cratchit, Cratchit's six children morphed into the dozen orphans the Bingles adopted during the course of the novel. Bingle was an old-school latitudinarian. Like Dickens he thought right religion a matter of deeds rather than doctrine, goodness rather than grace. "A thousand times" he said, "that if all men lived up to the teachings of 'A Christmas Carol' the world would be sweeter, happier, nobler, and the churches could be put to a better use than at present." He thought the "surest way to make good men out of all boys was to get at their hearts" while their souls were fresh and simple. Put *A Christmas Carol* and the New Testament in every boy's hand, and "they will create a religion that has something besides faith for a foundation."

The novel was a winter dessert, a fruit cake, the narrative more intoxicating than bourbon, the layers thick with candied fruit: fortunes lost, happiness won, lovers separated but joined at the altar, virtue tested but rewarded, improbable successes, sunny transformations, wealth and poverty, the deserving and the temporarily undeserving, jolly servants and fortunate orphans, Christmases past, present, and gloriously to come, and finally from the bottom of Santa's stocking an improbable heart-warming wonder, a sugarplum that enables the weary to imagine the hooves of Dasher and Dancer prancing across the tops of their lives. The book was corny and often poorly written, but just right for a snowy night's undemanding reading. It was a holly and mistletoe volume appealing to people at least seventy, but more than likely over eighty, who have aged beyond realism and ambition, who know eggnog to be headier than criticism but don't need to swallow either, wise people who realize that sentimental fabrications are more elevated and elevating than higher truths. Sometimes I think only the old are capable of being uncritically happy. Everyone else seems to enjoy frustration and the pleasures of discussing injustices so much that joy eludes them. My friend David and I, to bring Gilbert and Sullivan to mind, are two academics off from school. Our lyrical talents cannot match those of Yum-Yum, Peep-Bo, and Pitti-Sing, but words also make us gleeful. Last week David sent me his latest poem. Pooh-Bah wouldn't enjoy it, but certainly Mr. Bingle would. "I am a llama, / As is my mmomma. / Likewise my ppappa, / So pprim and so pproppa."

Money played a major role in the lives of McCutcheon's dramatis personae. In *Brewster's Millions*, the last novel I read, Money was the major character. Published in 1902, the novel and versions of the tale have been very popular. In 1906 an adaptation appeared on Broadway. Since then, a banker's dozen of film versions have appeared, the contents of the teller's drawer rising higher than those on the tray of any baker, renderings of Brewster's story having risen yeasty in India, Brazil, and China. At the start of the book, Monty Brewster and eight companions met in a friend's studio. Known as "The Little Sons of the Rich," they were young, enterprising, and reasonably "sure of better things to come." They were popinjays but not bounders. "A man," one of them remarked, "is known by the street that's named after him." Because of ongoing construction in New York, they nicknamed the newest member of the group Subway. Matters are only slightly different today on university campuses. Streets are not named for the wealthy, but for football and basketball coaches.

Monty's grandfather left him a million dollars, enough to guarantee a comfortable life. But then the long-vanished brother of Monty's mother, died and left Monty seven million dollars. However, the uncle despised Monty's grandfather and did not want his money tainted by that bequeathed by the grandfather. Consequently, he attached a condition to his will saying the seven million would go to his nephew only if Monty were penniless at the end of a year, that is, if he divested himself of every cent left to him by his grandfather. Moreover, Monty had to spend the money. He couldn't simply toss it out the window. Nor could he gamble recklessly. He had to avoid any dissipation that was not "ordinary." Moreover, he could not endow an institution or make large donations to charity, at least not beyond those made by other millionaires, the insinuation being that the wealthy were more parsimonious than generous.

Today ridding oneself of a million dollars is as easy as passing through the pick-up window at McDonald's and buying an Egg McMuffin. One hundred and nineteen years ago, it was an ordeal, complicated by interest, unexpected generosity, and bad investments surprisingly becoming good investments. Transforming a balance sheet into a wildly imbalanced sheet was extraordinarily difficult. To do so Monty left New York, hired a yacht for five months, and toured the Mediterranean. Accompanying him was an assortment of friends: the Sons, people whom he helped, people who wanted to help themselves to his fortune, and above all Peggy Gray and her mother. Peggy was the girl almost left behind. Although Monty did not realize it, he and Peggy had been sweethearts since childhood. When they were little, they read Oliver Optic's books in the garret of Peggy's mother's house. The name *Gray* suited Peggy, as it did the unassuming, often silent, qualities of decency, honesty, and love. Despite the millions, Virtue, of course, was rewarded as could be expected by anyone who read Optic's novels as I did as a young academic, not in an attic but in the basement under the rare book room of Baker Library at Dartmouth.

McCutcheon wrote more than forty novels. Initially I intended to read them all expecting they'd see me a long way toward one hundred and twenty, maybe beyond it. In order to participate in the narratives and relish the wealth of the main characters, I planned to spell the reading by buying lottery tickets. Never trust the artist, D. H. Lawrence said, trust the tale. Perhaps if I trusted the tale, I told Vicki, I'd win the lottery and "bring home the bacon," this despite our having given up eating pig. Of course, a million dollars would disappear quickly. Once the state and federal government sliced off their shares and we sent hunks to the children, Vicki and I'd be left with McMuffins, a good supply but McMuffins, nonetheless.

Despite deacidification the best laid bookish plans crumble. One morning after breakfast as I sipped Scottish tea before settling to read *Castle Craneycrow*, I suddenly realized that the two previous Sam Pickerings, my father and grandfather, died at eighty-one. In spite of having written twenty-five volumes of personal essays, my life is a closed book, rather several closed books. The pages are cut, but although I describe my doings, I'm not really in the paragraphs. Where I can be found is in my DNA. As my beginning was like those of Father and Grandfather, so I suspect my end will resemble their ends. Realizing that I had trotted past eighty and was cantering toward eighty-one, I decided it behooved me to post to the conclusion of this essay and declare, as an untrustworthy artist, that I had already reached one hundred and twenty.

If perchance I leap eighty-one, stay in the saddle, and bound into eighty-two, and if the leaves covering the yard, are not too exhaustingly deep, I may open my notebook and gallop forward to "Reading at One Hundred and Sixty." Equestrian matters were on my mind because I recently finished Clarence Edward Mulford's *Bar-20*, the first of twenty-five or so novels describing the exploits of Hopalong Cassidy. In 1906 Hopalong was not the avuncular William Boyd, attired in black and mounted on Topper the great white horse. He wasn't a stodgy upholder of law and morality whose only vice was a weakness for sarsaparilla. Instead, he was a twenty-three-year-old red-haired, loose-triggered cowpoke, an irresponsible rapscallion with a five hundred dollar reward on his head, a charming thug who "loved" ventilating cow punchers who offended him. Shot in the leg while foiling the assassination of his friend Sheriff Harris of Albuquerque, he walked with a limp. The horses he rode were four-legged cloudbursts or as he labeled one, a "wall-eyed, onery, locoed guide to Hades."

The only people able to read *Bar-20* without suffering narrative indigestion are those afflicted with the patience and immobility of old age and who, experiencing the pangs of senility, have suspended belief, and broken all critical yardsticks. The novel's pages are dyspeptic with flatulent dialect and gunfights between imbeciles in comparison to whom elementary school dunces look like geniuses. Even when shooting each other the cowboys resembled mischievous schoolboys. All had nicknames: Bigfoot, Tenspot, Waffles, Skinny, and Fat. Aristotle Smith played chess with empty and loaded cartridges. Salvation Carroll received his nickname "because he wasn't," and, of course, Cassidy, Hopalong because he was lame. Money was "mazuma." A badge was a license tag. Toads were warts, and Fleas, the name of a mangy yellow dog. Only rarely did a gunfight aspire to the literary. After Hopalong killed Dan a claim-jumper in Red Dog, one of the dead man's acquaintances said Dan "bought a bottle of ready-made nerve and went to his own funeral."

Most early westerns were at sea on the range. Because I didn't want the mental health of readers to resemble that of Dan, I abandoned the wide-open spaces to the deer and the antelope. However, once a reader starts trotting through books, tossing the reins of pages is impossible, and after I left the Bar 20, I joined Walter De La Mare's *Henry Brocken* on his travels through "Scarce-Imagined Regions of Romance." Henry's parents died just before his fourth birthday after which he lived with his aged Aunt Sophia. She was kind, but to her a child was something of "a little animal" to be fed and clad then ignored. As a result, for years Henry spent days and nights in what had been his uncle's library. He was an only child, but he was never lonely. Books were his companions. One blue March morning when a wind blew the trees of his aunt's woods about "in a pale-green tumult," he mounted his uncle's old mare Rosinante and "set out on a journey that has yet to come to an end." He rode into hills that bookish people recognize as both distant and immediate. Soon he met Wordsworth's Lucy Gray, Herrick's Julia, and Jane Eyre and her husband Mr. Rochester. Ahead stretched volumes of literary acquaintances, dusty but like holly ever green.

Books make a life, and before I finish my journey, I promise to introduce fancifully inclined readers to someone Brocken did not meet, the Countess Mara-Dafanda "familiarly and lovingly known in her own land as Countess Ted." During endless internecine Balkan wars, the countess's castle was demolished, her farmlands "pillaged," her "chests of gold" stolen, and as members of the Four Hundred said of the nouveau poor, she "didn't have a pot to piss in." Her actual fortune was a different sort. Her lips, an "uncommonly genteel tramp" noted, are "two of the most glorious rubies in the world." "Her eyes are sapphires that put to shame the rocks of all the Sultans; when she smiles, you may look upon pearls that would make the Queen of Sheba's trinkets look like chinaware; her skin is of the rarest and richest velvet; her hair is all silk and a yard wide; and, best of all, she has a heart of pure gold."

Alas, sometimes I think today's literary circus has lost two of its rings and all its elephants. No longer is the three-decker novel such stuff as dreams are made on. The Big Top has collapsed, and calliopes don't fill nights with music. Magicians have vanished. Rabbits live in hutches not top hats, and fat ladies have had bariatric surgery. String beans shovel lard into their frying pans and look like Anjou pears. No longer do gaggles of clowns pour out of small cars.

Cotton candy isn't pink, and Sailor Jack doesn't hand boxes of Cracker Jacks to children. Tony maidens don't carry ten steamer trunks with them onto ocean liners when they elope, and a boy's best college friend isn't a chum. No one slaps his thigh, jumps to his feet, and shouts "yowsir" when he hears "The Stars and Stripes Forever." Social gourmands have been weaned from Champagne and Baked Alaska onto diets of skim milk and honeydew. No longer do fashionable scribblers wrap gals in spangles and bows. No more do high born vamps kick up their heels, swing on trapezes, and tumble through pages like Slinkies. Edwardo who boasted in a romantic novel that he "loved a thing of beauty, were it a woman, a horse or a Mediterranean sunset" scrubbed his testimonial. He covered his roving eye with a patch and shortened his first name to Ed. Afterward he donned dungarees and becoming a gardener confined wandering to his yard. He bought a spade at Home Depot and at the cash register declared his admiration for Daphne, Sweet Cicely, Buttercup, Black-Eyed Susan, and pink-petaled Petunia, the flower next door.

# Who Am I Now?

I have long admired H.E. Bates and have read 15 of his novels. Recently I opened *The Poacher*. Immediately I noticed it was dedicated "To Sam." "Marvelous and miraculous," I said to Vicki showing her the inscription. "The book was published in 1935, six years before I was born. What a seer Bates was." "Oh, Sam," Vicki said. "The book wasn't dedicated to you. If it had been, the inscription would have read "To Sam, the Greatest Horse's Ass on the Planet." Although not an equestrian, Vicki has often compared me to the hindquarters of an equine, usually with affection and admiration, almost never critically. As people age and glance back through their decades, they often marvel at how various their years were. During silent arm-chair evenings, they realize they'd behaved like the Scarlet Pimpernel. Not only had they been here and there, but they'd been different people and perhaps different animals at disparate times. Life is fragmentary, and identity is fluid. Moreover, if a person outlasts his breath, he usually inhabits anecdotes and fragments of stories, the recollections of family, and if he wrote, in an occasional paragraph lively with the misremembered. In resuscitating the dead, it is better for a teller of tales to recall too little than too much. Most remembrances even those of the living are colored by quickening error.

In March *The Gate in the Garden Wall*, a collection of my essays, was published. The essays were docile, as becomes the thoughts of an aged man. Only two or three sentences were reptilian, their contents probably affected by an indiscriminate indulgence in television news and onion bhajis. In any case the eyes misread what the fingers write. "Yesterday I saw an announcement of your new book *The Gator on the Garden Wall*," an ancient acquaintance wrote from Assisted Living in Sarasota. "Last April a man from the Wildlife Commission removed a six-footer from the park behind the home. What excitement that caused! A racing of wheelchairs and hearts! In any case I've always hoped you would write a Florida book. I can't wait to read about the gator and have instructed Louise [the man's daughter] to order a copy for me."

As a person ages, books become his walker, and the ambulatory adventures of youth devolve into page turning. Thrice a week I ride my bicycle to the town Community Center where I paddle through three-quarters of a mile. The journey is short, about the distance I swim. The rush of cars along Route 275 makes me nervous, so I ride most of the way on a sidewalk, dismounting twice to cross streets. At night at home, I am intrepid. Two months ago, I accompanied Fred Birchmore as he rode *Around the World on a Bicycle*. What glorious experiences I had in Cairo and in cycling across the "Great Syrian Desert." On occasion I behaved like the sloping south side of a camel's hump, but I lived, really lived, and in the cool, quiet dark belonged to Robert Service's "race of men" who didn't "fit in," men who couldn't "stay still" but roamed "the world at will." Last weekend I explored the Caribbean with Richard Hughes and his bands of pirates and piratical children in *A High Wind in Jamaica*. Hughes began the novel in Wales but finished

146

it in Connecticut. "Like me," I thought. "I began elsewhere and now I am finishing in Connecticut."

In *The Solitary Summer* Elizabeth Von Arnim described reading books in places suited to their content. The conceit was pleasant but unworkable. *The Solitary Summer* was published in 1899 when Arnim was thirty-three. People my age are rational, not poetic, peripatetic readers. Thoreau, Arnim said, should be read outside. "He is a person who loves the open air and will refuse to give you much pleasure if you try to read him amid the pomp and circumstance of upholstery; but out in the sun, and especially by the pond, he is delightful." To appreciate the outdoors, one reads indoors. Inside, sheltered from the burning sun and away from mosquitos and no-see-ums, horseflies and springtime pollen, the natural nuisances that Thoreau rarely mentions, the reader has the leisure to ruminate. Arnim's prose is cosmetically smooth and appealing, but it lacks the slap of a palm chasing away sweat bees or the flick of fingers propelling ticks off ankles. The leech on the page differs from the leech in the groin. What octogenarian hankers to read *Tarzan* in a treehouse? To appreciate Ann Patchett's *Amazonia*, one should read her *State of Wonder* in a study blooming with chintz, far from the snagging lianas and howler monkeys of the rain forest. To straighten the legs of a child plagued by rickets, most responsible readers and parents, even when in Italy, don't embrace a remedy Norman Douglas mentions in *Old Calabria*, that is, visit a pet store, purchase a puppy, and after cooking it thoroughly in a saucepan, serve it to the youthful sufferer.

Many things that once shaped me Then do not shape me Now. Easter has almost vanished. The trumpets of white lilies that filled houses with perfume have withered and disappeared from dining room tables. Cultural myxomatosis has ravaged warrens of chocolate rabbits. A few remain but most are stale. Bunnies no longer bounce across lawns and scoot into briar patches serenaded by the glee of egg-hunting children. Roads are slaughterhouses, and the rabbits I see now don't shake their cottontails. They are granular clumps of fur and bone, and move only when a tire rolls over them. Of course, I have changed physically. Time has quarried the brawn that once turned my torso hard and lumpy. My skin sags, and the only "sinew" noticeable on my upper body is what Vicki dubs my "old man's muscle," a lemon-sized lipoma on the back of my right arm just above my elbow.

In 1979, the year after I began teaching in Storrs the *Journal of Modern Literature* published Robert Stallman's "That Crane. That Albatross Around My Neck: A Self-Interview." Bob was a well-known literary critic and had retired from the English Department at the university four years earlier. His most celebrated work was a biography of Stephen Crane, making him, as Carlos Baker my thesis advisor and dear friend wrote, the "world's foremost authority on what Crane wrote, thought, and did." Bob was smart and crusty, lively, opinionated, and rollicking with verbal fun. "How consumed did you become once you started to write your *Stephen Crane: A Biography*," the interview began. "How consumed?" Bob answered. "By gastritis, colitis, bursitis, phlebitis—all for the sake of Craneitis." I lack Bob's verve and critical stature, but I have written essays and books for more than fifty years. Occasionally, a few pages garnered attention, and if personal letters can be trusted, caused some literary readers to exclaim then smile. Bob died in 1982, and the interview was one of the last pieces he wrote.

I have reached the end page of my scribbling career. "Wouldn't it be amusing and maybe informative," I thought one evening, "to copy Bob and interview myself?" The first piece of mine published by the *Georgia Review* appeared in 1972, the last in 2018, and so I wrote the editor of the *Review* and proposed the interview. I said the interview would be "unbalanced" and promised not to sacrifice entertainment on the altar of truth. The editor wasn't interested. Times had changed, and Now wasn't hospitable to the thoughts of a traditional brick and adjective school essayist and teacher like me. The editor had not been in the post long enough to realize, as the ancient proverb puts it, "old camels carry the skins of young camels to the market." Still, the refusal was coated in the milk of magnesia of polite words and didn't cause any of the invigorating itises experienced by Bob. I simply muttered "shucks" and deleted his email.

As I turned to stand and leave the study, the telephone rang. Because calls like academic tastes have changed, I usually don't answer the phone. Almost never is a call personal. Usually, a crook is on the line. This time was not an exception, and the subject was familiar. "Hi, grandpa," a woe-begone voice said. "What? You're in jail again? You promised to reform," I replied. Before I got to the second syllable of promised, my "grandson" hung up. Sammy, my real grandson, was only eighteen months old. He chortles but doesn't talk a lot. Inexplicably the call cheered me. It was the sort of insignificance I'd mention in a self-interview. Just after I laid the receiver back in the cradle, the telephone rang again. My reaction resembled an echo, and without thinking I answered the call. "Hello," Ashok said, "this is Peter from Eversource Energy. How are you today?" "I am fine," I said. "What are you calling about, Peter?" Ashok paused before answering. Then he said, "nothing," soundly sad and wistful, too tired to continue talking. Before I could reply, the line went dead. That night a line from Von Arnim's *The Enchanted April* came to mind. In pondering her life, Lady Caroline, a beautiful and simultaneously reluctant and not so reluctant, socialite, declared, that it "suddenly seemed as if her life had been a noise all about nothing." Nothings are the heartwood of a person's days. Water and minerals may rush "vivaciously" through sapwood, but it is heartwood thick with resins and gums—ordinary doings—that shores up existence and keeps people on their feet.

Although age has stripped bounce from my stride, I haven't lost my affection for tedium. The pleasures of tediousness are not exciting, but they are real. Practically every day a nubbin of resin entertains me. At an ice cream social two weeks ago, a woman who studiously eschews graphic language said she hoped a national politician would spend his next life in Satan's microwave, referring to Gehenna as "H-e-double hockey stick." On Saturday I drove Vicki to Michaels to have a photograph enlarged. Aisles of the store were bazaars of artificial flowers: Irises, hydrangeas, daisies, sunflowers, pansies, tulips, lavenders, daffodils, roses, peonies, ropes of wisteria, and countless hybrids. The flowers were made out of paper, plastic, silk, and mystery cloths that looked like the remnants of pajamas. "Who buys these flowers?" I asked the clerk. "Lots of people," she replied. "But none of the blossoms are fragrant," I said. "That's not a problem," she said. "T. J. Maxx next door sells all sorts of perfumes. People go there, buy scents, and spray their flowers." "What?" I exclaimed. "And," the clerk continued, "no bugs."

Taking writing solemnly is debilitating. Rarely have books cured the lame or raised the dead. Only once has a poem changed a cannibal into a butterfly and never has anaphora caused a wart on a virgin's nose to sprout a ponytail of golden hair. Of course, bibliophobes argue that books have transformed herds of thoroughbreds into jackasses. I'm not sure. Generally, the tales I've heard describe the opposite: words conferring pedigrees upon donkeys. However, the accounts are so operatic and inspiring that they are probably apocryphal. In any case, I don't believe in literary miracles. I've grown flaccid and read more for statements light with helium than those earthbound with significance and moral uplift. In *The Enchanted Garden* Mrs. Fisher was stuffy, a character attribute responsible for memorable statements. To the manor born appealed to her more than to the manor earned. "Inheritance was more respectable than acquisition," she thought. She approved of inheritances because they implied fathers "in an age where most people appeared neither to have them nor to want them." Lengthy criticisms of life exhaust and irk me. I prefer single arrowhead sentences, assertions I remember long enough to quote--an example being a question gleaned from a letter in which an emeritus professor lamented a son's untoward conduct. "Why does being responsible and loving," she wrote, "often require forcefulness and momentary cruelty?" Unfortunately, the professor had not been retired long enough to shed the rhetorical elephantiasis caused by years of writing obscure and ostensibly witty literary analyses. "My son," she wrote, "resembles a cucumber. Persuasion does not affect him. I am trying to force his mind into the right frame." She did not elaborate further, but I suspect she threatened to disinherit him, money being the stepmother of morality. A sharper remark was Norman Douglas's judgment that "excess of sentiment, like all other intemperance, is the mark of that unsober and unsteady beast—the crowd." Or perhaps more memorable, "Beware the wrath of the lamb," a warning against allowing the soul to be "arbiter over reason." Douglas wrote better than he lived. I have lived better than I wrote. "I like that last line," Vicki said. "When you die, I'll have it engraved on your tombstone--A Man Who Lived Better than He Wrote."

# Bail

Vicki and I bailed on Thanksgiving. On the day before we bought a roasted chicken at Price Chopper for seven dollars. That was bird enough for us. On Thanksgiving afternoon Vicki cooked a vegetable mix of carrots, butternut squash, red onions, and red peppers. That night we ate dinner in the television room and watched "Royal Flying Doctor Service" on PBS. Midway through the episode Vicki served a strawberry-rhubarb pie which she bought at the Farmers' Market in June and then froze. We decorated our slices with a scoop of vanilla ice cream. We wanted the day to be a little festive, and that morning we tried to buy a bottle of Champagne. All the local liquor stores were closed, even those owned by Hindus. Consequently, we drank good, chlorinated water. However, the next morning liquor stores were open, and we purchased a bottle of Korbel, cheap but a suitable companion for leftovers.

We also plan to bail on Christmas at home. We won't tack a wreath to the front door or raise a tree in the living room. I won't hang stockings, make eggnog, or hear reindeer on the roof and angels singing on high. Generations of ornaments will remain boxed in the attic. They will miss their two weeks in the light, and I'll miss the happiness they shed throughout the house. They will be lonely and wail. I'll hear them and feel bad. Not seeing the Santa Claus that stood atop my first tree will sadden me, and the day will pass like a shadow. I won't experience Christmas morning's euphoria or the afternoon's melancholy sense of time passing. I won't become exasperated when Vicki peels wrapping paper off presents and folds the pieces to use another year.

I am gray. The corn tops aren't ripe, and the meadow isn't in bloom. Christmas Eve I'll probably weep silently for the old home "far away" in Tennessee which, rationally, I know exists no longer. "Happy are they who leave the scenes of early youth to the ministry of Time," Myrtle Reed wrote in *The Master's Violin.* "Going back, one finds the river a little brook, the long stretch of woodland only a grove in the midst of a clearing, and the upland pastures that once seemed mountains, are naught but stony, barren fields." Books proffer consolations. Most are simultaneously true and false, and all are fleeting. Although memory embellishes and Time diminishes the old home and old acquaintances, I miss them. At Christmas I suffer from an uncurable variant of "Lovesick Blues." Life would be easier if I sounded like I was from Nowhere. Never will I distill "Merry Christmas" from my speech and greet people with the social teetotaler's "Happy Holidays." "Mother always made a coconut cake," I'll say to Vicki. "Did I ever tell you that?" "Yes," Vicki will answer, "many times, every Christmas."

Even if they spend decades teaching at a single school, academics are nomads. They come from else-where's. Childhood companions are far away, and academics don't know people with whom they can naturally and spontaneously share memories. They learn about deaths not by walking downtown but by reading obituaries. There's no one with whom they can recollect "When you and I were young, Maggie."

After World War II, many D. P.'s or Displaced Persons settled briefly in rural Hanover County, Virginia. Most were Latvians. They did not stay long. After mustering energy and money, they moved to more congenial urban places. The behavior of the offspring of university teachers resembles that of Displaced Persons. They are D.C.'s, that is, Displaced Children. Only proximity links their parents to neighbors, not shared childhoods and adolescent friendships. Mind, not the tensile strength of emotion, forges the ties that bind their family to place. D.C.'s rarely escape becoming nomads. Because of their upbringings they don't think in terms of hometowns. After college they scatter imitating the movement of their parents. In a sense they bail, putting miles between them and the streets on which they grew up, making familial Christmases difficult and laborious. Although Francis lives only an hour away in Connecticut, Edward resides in South Carolina and Eliza in California. If they visited Storrs during the holidays, the zoos of animals which wandered the mantle and tabletops during past Christmases wouldn't recognize them. "Never move out of sight of your own smoke stacks," Mother told me. Bailing does not come easily to people living in the communities in which not only their parents but also their grandparents lived and died. To me, it comes too easily. Of course, bailing is never complete, no matter what a person may think. Three days after Thanksgiving. Edward's wife Erica telephoned. Sammy, our grandson, is almost a year old. For a while he has been saying "Ma Ma" and "Da Da," but then he said "Bubble" clearly. Immediately, Vicki left the house and bought a bottle of bubbly, this time not New York State plonk but expensive over the seas stuff, too good for us but right for a post-Thanksgiving Sammy memory.

Not until time kneecaps us will Vicki and I stop ambling. Thanksgiving morning we walked along the Fenton River past the old grist mill to the Beaver Pond. We met one other person, a man walking Annie, his black Lab. Annie was nine years old and overweight. "She's my best friend," the man said, "For Thanksgiving I bought a pumpkin pie, and when we return home I'll give Annie a big slice." Before dinner I wrote two condolence letters. "Shoveling on words," Vicki said. I write only widows because there are no widowers. Another friend's granddaughter had simultaneously gone off the shallow and deep ends. I took the woman to a dance when we were juniors in high school. We talked about books. She became a school teacher and since then we have corresponded occasionally. Alas, I didn't know what to write. It is too bad that like all other spiritual consolations "Trust in God" has been worn threadbare. While I sat at my desk, my old friend a red-tailed hawk perched on a limb outside the window. I asked her to suggest things to write. "You have a higher and better perspective than I do," I said, she didn't answer but instead fluffed the feathers on her breast and flanks which, if I understood the greater world better, might have been a reply. That night during the early morning hours a light snow fell, and while I ate breakfast, heavy showers of grackles blew back and forth across the yard, gathering in trees then suddenly falling and rising through the hard winter air. The backs of the necks of the males were purple and iridescent, their beauty something I ignored during summers.

My nights are more intriguing than my days. At times I'd like to close my dreams like the covers of a book, but I cannot. Not long after Thanksgiving, I felt the blankets on my bed rippling like wavelets on the surface of a pond. Above me hovered a thin black silk cloth. I couldn't tell whether the cloth was descending or rising. Whatever the truth, I bailed and woke gasping for air. Although the dream puzzled me, I didn't think much about it. Dawn was breaking, and I looked out the bedroom window. A yearling deer raced along the fence in the side yard, gamboling in the joy of living. Later it joined a rangale of does grazing the front yard. I didn't ponder the dream because the imagined doesn't attract me as strongly as it once did. I'd rather watch a murmuration of blackbirds sweeping and falling in waves over the sheep barn and behind the silos on the university farm.

Of course, people, especially the learned, unendingly study the undesigned and impose human meaning on the natural. Last year an old acquaintance attended a performance of "The Reindeer People: a Folk Epic" staged at a university in his home town. The presentation lasted seventy minutes, but, my correspondent judged, "seemed endless." Eight people appeared on the stage. They wore brown suits ostensibly the shade of the velvet that covers the developing antlers of reindeer. The night was humid, and "against all expectation I dreamed that at the end of the show the performers would behave like mature reindeer, shed their costumes, and gallop off stage wearing Bermuda shorts and Hawaiian shirts." It was, my acquaintance emphasized "that kind of evening." The performance consisted of "primitive" chanting punctuated not by words and grammar but by sounds made by reindeer: grunts, barks, snorts, heavy breathing, and "the inelegant expulsion of rectal breezes." Throughout the show, one performer clicked castanets, mimicking the snapping made by the tendons in the legs of reindeer as they walked.

"Call me Oscar the Grouch," my correspondent ended, "but I kept hoping Mr. Snuffleupagus would rumble out of the wings and wagging his trunk drive the manqué Laplanders into another, preferably distant and frozen, anthropologically receptive compound."

Last Wednesday at dusk I shoveled mulch around the boxwood in front of the house. Deer chewed the yews that once flourished there into a mesh of barren twigs and skewers. In September I ripped the yews out of the ground and planted box. "Deer-proof," a university gardener told me. The afternoon was icy. Earlier when I asked Vicki if she were cold, she said, "I won't be warm again until April." While I spread mulch, a frigid rain began to fall. "Damn," I thought, "Thanksgiving was only a starter. I'd like to bail out of winter itself." However, that was only a before-tea thought. Early morning had been lovely. A thready frost glazed Horsebarn Hill. Mist pooled up from nearby valleys and softened the bristly sides of gullies. Here and there tousles sifted loose and drifted away as sunlight parted the damp like a silver blade. In the distance ridges rose blue one behind another. From the edge of a wood crows called, the sound not disturbing but familial and homey.

The number of things to be escaped are legion, especially as a person ages. Actually nuisances increase as dementia begins to cloud reason, a prime example being the attention of "benevolists" who rip at bank accounts of the elderly. Every day I receive a stern looking card masquerading as an official notice. Printed on the front are generally "Registered To" and "Release Code," the first followed by my name, the second by a mash of numbers. Postage for the most recent card was paid in Palatine, Illinois and was supposedly sent only to residents of Tolland County,

Connecticut. Sponsored by "GoHealth," it urged me to call an 844 number for a free "Medicare Review." It also listed several possible big bucks savings. I crumple such mailings and pitch them into the recycle bin. But I fret that in the future when the "GoHealth" of my brain has become "GoneHealth," I'll mistake an ad for an official notice and respond to its blandishments. Still, hooks baited with dollars probably won't seduce me. Habit is an effective prophylactic. Most things for which I wished I possessed on the page. A book life is wealth enough, and for me the appeal of wildflowers has always been stronger than grocery carts of green paper.

I have bailed from many contemporary knick knacks. I don't heed the jabber of public talk: educational, athletic, political, and religious among choruses of others. In J. B. Priestley's *The Magicians*, Sir Charles Ravenstreet invites a trio of eccentric characters into his home Broxley Manor. Having recently resigned from New Central Electric, Ravenstreet has neither family nor career and is, in a sense, free. For years he lived according to the code of corporate expectation, his days marked by the mechanical tick tock of anesthetizing conformity. From the magicians' point of view, he lived by dead time rather than "time alive." In the novel, the magicians breathe vitality into the bones of Ravenstreet's existence. In the process they disrupt convention. One of the magicians Nicholas Perperek so upsets a coroner's inquest that a leathery magistrate sends him to a police station. When Perperek vanishes, Inspector Triffett is mystified. As the unexpected makes most people uncomfortable, so Perperek's disappearance upsets Triffett's spiritless allegiance to prosaic order. Consequently, he visits Broxley Manor and grills Ravenstreet. If one of the magicians, he says, "should get in touch with you, Sir Charles, will you promise to let me know?" Ravenstreet smiles, shakes hands with the policeman, and bails, replying, "Certainly not, Inspector," the answer not negative but positive, being a rejection of smothering compliance and an affirmation of idiosyncratic life.

Although "certainly not" has become an increasingly appropriate response to much I hear or see, I have not abandoned curiosity. However, matters that intrigue me now differ from those that elicited momentary notice in the past, that is, the "determined ignorance" of the public classes. What I am presently curious about is sensible, personal, and wholesomely different. For example, last evening after turning off the television, I spent a goodly portion of the time while climbing the stairs to my bedroom wondering how many bananas I'd eaten in my life. Once in bed I pondered changes caused by the virus. No longer do Jehovah's Witnesses knock at the door. Now they mail letters, always handwritten and punctuated correctly. Two days ago Camille wrote me from Willimantic. Accompanying her letter was a tract, "What is the Kingdom of God?" "It shows," she said, "how living by God's standards helps you find lasting love, happiness, and security." "Oh, Lord," I thought and fell asleep. That night I dreamed I had a stroke. "What does that mean?" Vicki asked the next morning. "I don't care," I said. "Aren't you curious?" she said. "No," I said. "So long as I can wiggle my ears and roll my tongue, I'm in good shape." "What?" Vicki said.

Camille's letter was an exception. Only rarely do I receive first class mail. Most is underclass. Would that I could avoid receiving broadsides like the one that recently informed me that "Icelandic Haddock

Fish" had arrived in Storrs and despite being flown 2,700 miles from Reykjavik to New York then driven 140 miles across Connecticut, went well with "crispy fries." "Life Is Worth Hearing," an advertisement from the Hear Again Center declared. "Rubbish," Josh said. "The poor of hearing are often rich in understanding. Speech deceives, and like the daughters of Achelous seduces and corrupts. Earwax is the great God's tympanic prophylactic." Someday maybe cerumen will block verbal pop-ups like "I'm taking it one day at a time." Last week I heard it in the waiting room of a doctor's office. On a nurse's asking about his health, a patient used the banality. "What a fool," a woman sitting across from me said. "If that man just lives one day at a time, why is he here? Doctors are in the business of extending life. The halfwit is in the wrong place. His appointment should be with a mortician."

Awards and flashy unnecessary possessions don't blind me. In April I'll buy urea-based fertilizer for the boxwood. For myself I won't purchase anything. The old clothes I wear in which to work and to amble about town suit me. Still, I occasionally doubt myself. I fear that bailing out of the appurtenances decorating capitalist society may be an indulgent compensation, producing an inflated sense of moral superiority at a time when I am shrinking and becoming physically inferior. As a person ages, fallings from him increase. Losing spring in the legs is as natural as the loss of spring in the heart, that is, withdrawing from the celebratory, be that Thanksgiving or New Year's Eve. "Little is worse," Josh says, "than the dead feeling of waking up alive yet again."

For some time, Josh has bailed ostentatiously which actually may be a form of not bailing. Last

February he wrote an editorial in which he suggested changing Presidents' Day to Almost Presidents' Day. "The leaden dollar bill headmen bore me," he testified. "I have seen enough Washingtons, Jeffersons, Jacksons, and Lincolns." In the editorial he admitted that because he was susceptible to cupidity a handful of McKinleys would not depress him. Nevertheless, he wrote, "how interesting it would be to celebrate Lewis Cass who lost to Zachary Taylor in 1848, Horace Greeley whom Grant defeated in 1872, and Coolidge's opponent in the 1924 election John W. Davis. Groceries could feature foods the Sell-By dates of which had expired and haberdashers, discontinued lines of clothing. Hand-shakers might scrub snake-oil off their palms, and the old gray mare just might become what she used to be."

Changing reading is also natural. Oldsters do not have the minds or arms to lift hefty volumes. Occasionally one reads an article in which a retired teacher is supposedly rereading all Shakespeare's plays. The assertion is a lie, one repeated so often in university propaganda magazines that it smacks of myth. Usually, the articles quote former students whose minds have so softened that they recollect their college days with uncritical fondness. Because they did not understand their classes, they think the fault in themselves not in their teachers. Now with platitudinous grace they praise stupendous old bores, thinking them characters and assuming incomprehensible lectures Delphic rather than moronic. "She is forever frozen in time as the professor who changed how I think about life," the student writes. "Does she still ride a bicycle around the university and reread Jane Austen's novels every year?"

In truth bicycles are rusting in the dark backs of

garages, and old teachers are not reading anything. Instead, if they can hear, they listen to their mates reciting the side effects of the medicines they bolt like peanuts. Sometimes an obituary claims that a literary lady died half an hour after reading *War and Peace* for the 4<sup>th</sup> time. In truth after being freed from the shackles of academic schedule the old gal spent her evenings shoeless and happily thoughtless, resting her feet on an ottoman hoping the swelling would go down and reading shelves of The Bobbsey Twins, the fifty volumes published before 1957, none remastered out of entertainment into higher truths prescribed for contemporary social ills.

I follow the pattern. As roasted chicken suited my Thanksgiving, so I have bailed from reading massive books heavily seasoned with thought and awash in impenetrable sentences. I'm not attracted to popular multi-decker biographies, say those of Ulysses S. Grant or Robert E. Lee. Single sentences hold my attention longer than paragraphs. "Every man has some vice or other, even if it is only being good," I recently read. "Hmm," I thought. "That's me." Happily, the hero of the book had two vices, "poker and tobacco." He also had two humanizing susceptibilities, one to the seductive dreams of *Treasure Island*, the second to American girls whose skins have "the bloomy olive pallor of a young peach" and whose eyes "are as heavenly blue as a rajah's sapphire." In truth what attracts me are not the eyes of damsels frolicking in the money but the lives of Carolina wrens, "the little birds with the big voices." A pair lives in my brush pile. Many mornings while making breakfast, I watch them digging and scratching through the litter under the lilacs outside the kitchen window. Their quick, peppy, foraging makes me smile and sweetens my granola.

Hazlitt's "On Going A Journey" was an apologia for bailing. "We go on a journey," he wrote, "chiefly to be free of all impediments and of all inconveniences; to leave ourselves behind, much more to get rid of others." "Oh!" he hymned, "it is great to shake off the trammels of the world and of public opinion—to lose our importunate, tormenting, everlasting personal identity in the elements of nature, and become the creature of the moment, clear of all ties." In an inn where no one knows them, people, he wrote, can "baffle prejudice and disappoint conjecture; and from being so to others, begin to be objects of curiosity and wonder even to ourselves. We are no more the hackneyed commonplaces that we appear in the world." How wonderful to shake off the algorithms of advertising and no longer be thought a financial opportunity by salesmen hawking medical insurance. How marvelous to dodge the darts of solicitations and the bludgeons of catalogues—simply to be "clear" if only for a moment. Of course, bailing is always short-lived. Hazlitt was an essayist. The snake may shed his skin and the harlequin leopard disguise his spots, but the essayist is a less adaptable animal. He may drop his pencil and hesitate to retrieve it, but he will eventually reach down, seize it, and resume scribbling. "Essayists," my friend Josh once said, "rarely stop filling holes that pock their days, especially during the winter of their lives. Awareness that patches are ephemeral does not bother them." As could be expected, Hazlitt's journey didn't end in a lonesome valley but publicly in an essay published in 1822 in the *New Monthly Magazine*.

In spite of the ridges and deep arroyos that separate travelers from their pasts, rarely are people clear of all ties. Nor do they wish to be. At their quickening best ties remind people that they lived. Vicki and I spent the first year of our marriage in Latakia, Syria. We were gloriously happy. But like most of our decades together that time has vanished. When asked about Syria I am usually speechless, and I doubt that we were actually there. But then someone writes me, and for a moment memory thrusts through the winter of my years like the first green sprouts of daffodils pushing snow aside in the spring. Last week the son of a "girl" I taught at Tishreen University in 1980 wrote me. The man's mother became an English teacher and emigrated to Canada where my correspondent was born. Now he, too, teaches English. "Nineteen-eighty was a scary time," the man wrote, saying that his mother remembered the Sunni-Alawite tensions "very well." When she left Syria, "she left a big part of herself" there, especially "her entire family." She misses, the man continued, "the neighborly, folksy hospitality, the extended domestic life, and the beautiful beach and countryside." After leaving, she visited Syria only twice "both times before the war." As I read the man's email, I wondered about the fates of my students during the war. "So many people have wept for Syria," I said to Vicki. "How unspeakably sad. There are places to which a person unexpectedly returns but returns to only in imagination. Through the eye of the present such memories are often tormenting. It's probably better for the spirits and health of the elderly to bail from everything." "Bail from most things like the advertisement from the medical pharmacy peddling catheters and reading like a notice from a shoe store saying, 'One size does not fit all,'" Vicki said. "But don't bail from all life until the undertaker gives you a julip cup of methanol."

Good advice spoils quickly. "Some wit," Myrtle Reed wrote, "has said that the worst vice in the world is advice, and it is quite true that one ignorant though well-meaning person can sometimes accomplish more damage in a short time, that a dozen people who start out for the purpose of doing mischief." I try to avoid inadvertent mischief by not giving advice. However, bailing from proffering advice is difficult. No matter a person's seclusion, the intrusive will discover him and ask advice. Instead of leading an anchoritic existence in a serpent-infested desert cave, a person can escape unwanted inquiries by becoming known for foolish or memorable advice. At my age no matter the speed one discards the mail, conversation about deafness is repetitious and callousing. Four days after I "heard" from Hear Again, a casual acquaintance wrote Josh. The man complained about losing hearing and asked Josh to recommend a hearing aid. I am afraid Josh lost control of his pencil. "Don't worry about the hardening of your cochlea," Josh wrote. "It's a blessing. What people under fifty say is always trite, uninteresting, or mendaciously self-serving. For their part people over fifty are incurably repetitious. What you hear or mishear them say once, you'll hear again. But if you must purchase a hearing device, get one big as a turnip. Don't pay a fortune for an invisible pissant bug-like thing that dogs are fond of eating. Buy a trumpet. You won't mislay it. People will notice it and assume you're handicapped. Dolts will step out of your path, and naïve Samaritans will escort you to the front of queues particularly if you occasionally feign a hip-smashing stumble."

A regimen of travel books that transport readers over strange seas does not break the ties that bind a person to bed before ten o'clock. Even the most adventuresome writers who scour the world for excitement and scorn the everyday are ultimately commonplaces. Condolences must be written, pills taken, and physicians consulted. In December one sends Christmas cards to people whom he has not seen in years and will never see again. A person may eat chicken on Thanksgiving and not raise a tree in his living room on Christmas, but if he thinks he can slip the ordinary ties of life and escape himself he is deluded. Last week I went to a doctor's office. The office was crowded, so I sat and waited to sign in. When my turn came, I stood and walked toward the registration desk. "Mr. Pickering, you can sit back down," the receptionist said, "I've already signed you in." "What?" I said, "this is only the second time I've been here." "Mr. Pickering," the woman said, "we know you." Three days later in the locker room of the community gymnasium, a naked stranger asked me, "Did you get to your home in Nova Scotia this summer or did the virus stop you?"

Last weekend Vicki and I ate breakfast at the Wooden Spoon in Ashford, a place where I don't know and have never known anybody. While we were waiting for our order, a man whom I thought I'd never seen before came over to our table "What are you writing nowadays?" he asked. I was startled and stuttered weakly. "Nothing much," I said, "a piece on bailing out of things." "I'll bet it will be good," the man said. "Life is the sum of trifles." "Or" I said, "the absence of them." "That, too," the man responded then said, "I know who killed the great speckled bird. It was a duck hunter in South Carolina, the biggest contributor to Ducks Unlimited in the state, not a member of some post-Christian tabernacle." "Oh," I replied, after which the man nodded, then before he walked away said, "Enjoy your breakfast. We are eating almost the same thing, eggs sunny side up, hash browns, and pumpernickel. The only difference is that I'm having bacon, and you, patty sausage." Later I remembered the man. Years earlier he stopped Vicki and me while we were walking our dogs on the campus. He informed us that "Light My Fire" was written by the cadaver of an unrepentant reprobate buried during a icy winter. "John didn't get things quite right," the man said. "Jesus is not simply the door. He is The Doors." "On day leave from the asylum," Vicki said after the man disappeared. "On a bench somewhere we'll find his white sport coat, its wrap around arms untied."

On the Wednesday after breakfast at the Wooden Spoon was my yearly eye examination. For the aging, doctors' appointments are frequently the stuff out of which fantasies are made. The night before the examination I dreamed about the courtship of a nice man and a blind girl. The romance was a fairy tale sweet with love which led to a marriage iced with lasting happiness. One tale often evokes others, and while I sat in the ophthalmologist's waiting room, stories were on my mind and tongue. "Have you noticed that all the people who appear in the pictures in the Optical Shop are wearing glasses," I said, addressing a stranger sitting beside me reading *People*. "Isn't that odd? Do you suppose the lenses are magical?" The woman glanced at me then quickly looked away. But then she surprised me, turned back, and smiling said, "You're Sam Pickering. Aren't you? What are you writing now?"

On Monday the Hammacher Schlemmer Christmas catalogue arrived. It contained a madhouse of other-worldly creatures. For $99.95 the jolly old elf could give Momma "The Hypnotic Jellyfish Aquarium." "Two synthetic jellyfish" lived in "the LED lighted desktop aquarium." They "provided

mesmerizing ambiance just like their real counter-
parts." An array of lights caused these two members
of the Cnidaria phylum to float gently in the tank and
glow yellow, purple, blue, and red. If jellyfish frightened Momma, she could purchase a two pack of sea
horses for $9.95. If she bought four packs, she'd could
name them after St. Nick's antlered horses: Dasher
and Dancer, Prancer and Vixen, Comet, Cupid,
Donner and Blitzen. If the children nestled in their
beds ever saw "The RC Color Changing Chameleon,"
they wouldn't dream of sugar plums and years later
their teeth wouldn't resemble diminutive coal mines.
Eight inches long and magnetic, the Chordata's
tongue opened and shut like a telescope and a savvy
herpetologist could easily manage it from a hundred
feet away. The chameleon was a gourmand and
would not have bailed out of Thanksgiving. When
it snatched one of the "food" tokens that accompanied its purchase, its eyes and back changed colors.
Unfortunately it needed a course in table manners
and while eating set a bad example for children by
making "cooing, munching, and swallowing sounds."
"What next?" I said to Vicki. "Something familiar,"
she said. "The children asked me what to get you
for Christmas. Since you never want anything, how
about the jellyfish?" "Help," I said and went outdoors.
Juncos and titmice hopped and spun in the air like
ballerinas, and squirrels fanned their tails and chased
each other into arabesques.

169

# California Christmas

California is not Connecticut. When Vicki and I stepped off the plane in Palm Springs, Eliza handed us vegan pastrami sandwiches. We were hungry, and the "pastrami" was toothsome. It was mid-afternoon in Southern California, but to make a six o'clock flight from Hartford to Dallas, we'd gotten up at 1:30 in the morning. Roads were icy, and the minutiae of locking down the house sapped hours and spirits. The journey was ordinary and tedious. I'd booked tickets in July, selecting aisle seats. A week before we flew, American Airlines changed one of our return flights pinching us into middle seats. Afterward they offered to upgrade us for a price to seats comparable to the ones I'd initially booked. On the leg from Dallas to Palm Springs, a woman sitting next to me described her sick brother-in-law. He'd refused to be vaccinated and caught covid. "We almost lost him," she said. "Too bad," I thought, "pruning nincompoops helps evolution." "And my sister won't get the shots," the woman continued. "She says we don't know what's in them." "Little green dragons that convince good Christians to join the Temple of Set," I said, provoking an odd look from the woman and ending the conversation.

The trip to California had been years coming. Vicki and I adore Eliza, but we did not visit her when she lived three years in Germany. Neither did we visit when she worked in New York or when she went to school an hour and a half away in Boston. When she was little, we dropped her at camp in Maine in June and did not see her until seven weeks later. Other parents acted differently. They telephoned and appeared unexpectedly at the camp. I cannot explain our behavior. Vicki and I are strong-willed. Did we worry about being intrusive or domineering? Maybe we loved too much. Whenever Eliza left Storrs after a holiday at home, we cried. Maybe we were too weak to see her then shoulder the immediate sadness of being aware of her absence. People claim that they dislike solitude, but life is calmer if one is alone. Worries about the distant don't disturb like those focusing on the immediate. Speculation is misty and easier on nerves than clarity. For six years I resisted invitations from Eliza and Travis her husband to visit them in California. Becoming eighty softened me, and Vicki and I agreed to spend Christmas week in Palm Springs. Eliza organized our days, gathering family members and planning excursions. I opened my wallet and rented a house for Eliza and Travis, Francis, his friend Eddie, and Edward, Erica and their one year old boy Sammy Pickering. I also reimbursed people for their expenses: flights, car, food and drink, tickets of sundry sorts, etc. One morning I started to calculate the amount I spent, but I soon stopped. Christmas may be a commercial holiday, but the heartfelt is not a dollar and cent matter.

Vicki and I stayed in Old Ranch Inn, a one-story downtown hotel built in 1930 in Spanish style. Eight rooms surrounded a heated pool. Above and across the pool from the door to our room and only a small trek away for the telescoping eye loomed the San Jacinto Mountains. Throughout the day sunlight washed across them and their appearance changed. In late afternoon they looked like the chin of an old man gravelly with psoriasis, On bright mornings they were lemony and appealing. When a shadow from a cloud bathed them, they turned purple. At times snow drifted down ridges like wisps of hair breaking from brushing and combing. A kitchen was attached to our room, and we ate breakfast there, drinking tea and feasting on raisin bran and bananas, hard and green the way I like them. Once or twice I took the family to lunch, but mostly we ate in "The House." Eliza and Travis prepared meals: mystery "meatballs," tacos with soy chorizo, roasted sweet potatoes and carrots, cauliflower, and dishes strange with tofu, farro, chickpeas, and lentils. Once we had a leek and shitake stuffed seitan log smothered in white bean and sage gravy. Despite being told the ingredients, I had no idea what I was eating or how to taste it. We grazed on green salads loaded with goat cheese, dried cranberries, pecans, endive, and honey crisp apples. For dessert Travis made apple and blueberry crumble, and Vicki emptied a suitcase which she had transformed into a bakery. At home she packed it with Viennese crescents, iced sugar cookies, logs of chocolate refrigerator cookies, and loaves of bread: pumpkin, cranberry-orange, and brandied apricot. For liquids, people swilled good faucet water and bottles of Georgian wine, this last a drink Travis and Eliza became fond of during a three-week hiking trip. For conventional palates, we purchased red wine.

On Christmas Eve, Eliza served eggnog, a mule-kicking blend of rum, bourbon, and brandy tempered by eggs, confectioner's sugar and dollops of heavy cream. For my part age has made me abstemious, and aside from a welcoming cup of eggnog, I only drank the occasional beer, very occasional and very weak. There was a single exception. One morning

Francis bought a chocolate bar at the Lighthouse Dispensary and Lounge. Mint and another herb that was once illegal flavored the bar. Although age tempers appetite, it also creates scoffers. No one reaches eighty without realizing that the effects of laws are mixed and that many are fashioned by and for the benefit of imbeciles. The bar cost thirty dollars, more than any chocolate I'd ever munched. In younger, roaming days, I enjoyed sinking my teeth into the unknown, usually to the accompaniment of self-celebratory gusto. As could be imagined, afterward the rumblings and explosions abdominal were phenomenal. Nevertheless such zestful dietary matters were quickly forgotten. Indeed the mystery foods scoured my innards and kept me trim. I sampled Francis's bar announcing that I was sure sweets brewed in "conventional" Palm Springs wouldn't affect a seasoned traveler like me. I was wrong. It was the worst chocolate I ever ate. The hunk made me dizzy and prone to using overly-ripe adjectives to describe the debris gurgling below my guzzle pipes. I'd have been better off chewing mephitis cabbage rabe.

Dinners at the house were light and happy. People told corny jokes. A cheese monger's business was failing, Travis recounted, but then his factory burned down transforming the leaky roof and empty vats into de Brie. I didn't tell jokes, but I sang a ditty that J. B. Priestley's old vaudevillian Timmy Tiverton taught me: "You can't give Father any cockles; / You can't give Mother any gin; / Auntie's a sport, / But don't give her port, / You never know what she'll begin...."
One night everyone but me watched "The Matrix" on television. I went into Eliza's and Travis's bedroom and fell asleep. Their dog Sisko joined me. Sisko is an odd mix, probably of whippet and chihuahua. He

also avoids people other than his owners. He fancied me, however, and joining me in bed fell asleep with his muzzle on my collarbone. Another night while sampling guacamole before dinner, I changed my forename from Samuel to "The Truth." Moreover I did so without benefit of Christening by alcohol. At dinner and after a pitcher of wine from Tbilisi, people agreed the change was not only fitting but becoming, especially for an essayist who believes that dollops of truth make the fictional palatable and believable.

Of course, gentlemen eschew programmatic truthfulness. Veracity is inhumane. It grinds compassion into frass, blasts friendships and community, destroys gaiety and charm, and gelds fantasy. It is a high alkaline detergent that bleaches conversation and reduces stories to abrasive moral dish towels. However, the higher the caste, the weaker the lye, and the more wrinkled and genteel the conduct. While on the topic of nomenclature, I must add that oldsters often change Christian names into sobriquets more comfortably pagan. This generally occurs when the grasshopper becomes a burden and men consign three-piece suits to the moths and start wearing tracksuits or hospital Johnny's. An old academic comrade, raised in a palazzo in Texas but now camping in assisted living in Massachusetts, insists that the staff address him as "Cactus."

Like that of most people of a certain age, my acquaintance is mixed. It is, however, tossed slightly higher, seasoned a shake more, and contains a few more croutons than the everyday lettuce wedge. After their silver cords frayed and they graduated into nursing homes, two of my former compatriots changed their first names, both to the vegetable, one becoming known as Kale, the other as Broccoli.

Names have always been fluid. Before he became a poet, T. Kilgore Splake, for example, was Thomas Hugh Smith. Changing a name doesn't always reflect diminution or loss of reason as does my friends' embracing the kingdom Plantae. Sometimes it signals accretion. Today it is common to read about a person who is not singular but plural, an individual who is not one but a group of individuals, not a partner in a mixed doubles team but the entire team itself or perhaps several teams compounded. An adjustment of titles generally accompanies marriages of polygyny and polyandry. Gone are Mr., Mrs., Miss, and Ms. Replacing them is Mx.

Before I flew to Palm Springs, Ernie an old friend telephoned to wish me Merry Christmas. The conversation was the occasion of his recounting the antics of our college days. All his recollections were humorous, and none were discreditable. "You have always been the most responsible friend I have," Ernie said, "but when you walked out of a room, no one ever knew what you were going to do." The person Ernie described rarely appears nowadays. He was just one of several me's. All people are they's, behaving one way at twenty and another at fifty. The seventy-year-old isn't the eighty year old. Each individual is a group. Everyone is Mx. Indeed a reading of the Bible popular with Holiness prelates argues that Jesus's feeding the five thousand with five loaves and two fish was metaphorical, not actual. According to this interpretation the multitude consisted of all the individuals "inhabiting" a single being. Moreover, as a unitarian wag put it, eating the two fish and the bakery of loaves at a sitting must have given Jesus's dinner companion at Bethsaida indigestion, if not a windy case of divine afflatus. "If that interpretation becomes widespread,"

Josh said. "Not only will it give biblical exegetes the hives but it will wreck the economies of bakeries and fish markets."

Palm Springs is hot tub country. Behind "Eliza's house" was a pool. At one end was a tub. Only once had I been in a hot tub. That occurred thirty years ago during my single previous trip to California. Because my host was the Stanford Medical School, I abandoned worries of percolating effluvia. When in California, vacationers often behave as they assume natives do tasting wares sold at dispensaries and puddling about in hot tubs. Several of our group soaked before dinner, and to fit in I joined them. Besides bacteria no longer bother people who have experienced the eczema of three score and twenty years. I used the tub only once. Entering was easy. Getting out was difficult. I've become shaky especially when putting weight on my right leg. To extricate myself, I stood, leaned over the lip of the tub, and rolling onto grass, pushed myself off the ground—an inelegant itchy exit that didn't bear repeating.

For two summers after Mother died and before his own death, Father spent a fortnight with us in Vicki's house in Nova Scotia. After dinner he sat in a rocking chair by the wood stove in the kitchen and read to the children. He made memories, not for the children because they were too young for momentary experiences to become permanent. He made them for the remnant of his life and for me. Life is repetitious. In part our family gathered in Palm Springs to celebrate the first birthday of Little Sammy Pickering, Edward and Erica's Christmas present of a year ago. We cuddled Sammy and read to him. We helped him "walk" around tables and chairs holding edges and arms. We told him all sorts of things and described our hopes for him, dreams really, none of which he will remember. We fashioned memories for ourselves, for me who didn't simply resemble Father but who was Daddy approaching the end of his life, then for Vicki and Erica, but mostly for Edward who in some sentimental mood in the future will recall Palm Springs, his child, and his aging father, Time behaving as it always does, sawing backward and forward, forward and backward.

The house rented for Eliza was one-story and typical of an undistinguished, indeed faceless, upper middle-class suburb. Conveniently the house was a mile from Old Ranch Inn and downtown Palm Springs. Surrounding the property was a nine-foot-tall hedge of Indian laurel. In the city's wealthiest neighborhoods hedges were so thick that they functioned as stage curtains obscuring costly real estate props. In front of the hedges including the one surrounding Eliza's comparatively modest rental, appeared a medallion. Printed in white on a red background was "Armed Response Security 24/7." In fact, looking like cub scout merit badges security company signs decorated the shoulders of home driveways: Protection Inc., Desert Alarm Inc., Maxwell, Maximum Security, PSS or Personalized Security Service, Edison, "Patrolled by" Serna & Associates, Command 1 Security, ISMG Armed Patrol, PFL, and "Intelligent Premier Security," among a troop of others. There was such variety that I suspected one or two companies monopolized home security and doled out different signs to make the burglars fear that armed guards were always on the lookout.

Old Ranch Inn was on the edge of downtown, a quick amble from the Palm Springs Art Museum. The museum was uncluttered, an oasis apart from people milling along Palm Canyon Drive. Although I'd never been to Palm Springs, my visit to the museum fell into a pattern. Perhaps being away from home insured my behavior would be familiar. Be that as it may, in museums I always select a painting which I'd steal if hedges of convention and incapacity didn't "fence me in," as Bing Crosby put it. Lurking within aged adults who lead dutiful lives is a dram of intoxicating antisocial admiration for outlaws, for people unlike themselves who embraced temptation. In museums I usually choose an ordinary painting, often a landscape that pulls vision from the self and encourages it to roam. In Palm Springs I stole James Swinnerton's "Smoke Tree and Salton Sea." In the middle foreground appeared a smoke tree and a low scrub of bushes. To reach the Salton Sea the viewer had to wend through the foreground and behind the tree, something perhaps too easy because clouds of purple didn't billow from the tree confusing yet enticing. If American Airlines did not overcharge for extra luggage and I was grandfather to a school-house of children, I might also have taken Germaine Richier's bronze "Large Horse with Six Heads." The sculpture directed sight inward, rather than outward, to nightmares corralled in jagged angles of the mind. At its best the sculpture would disturb lazy sleep and awaken the imagination, something fairy tales do at their startling best.

In a park across from the entrance to the museum loomed "Forever Marilyn," a twenty-six-foot-tall steel and aluminum stature of the Marilyn Monroe of "The Seven Year Itch." Monroe stood on a sidewalk, famously trying to control her dress as it sailed above her knees blown by gusts of air escaping from a subway grate. The statue was prurient.

When tourists walked beneath it and looked up, they saw Monroe's white cotton underpants, a sight that would have been pornographic if it were not banal. "What do you suppose, Hanes, Bali, Fruit of the Loom?" I heard a woman say. Nearby gapped a large deep sandbox. Crawling through it across the San Andreas Fault were nine of David Cerny's fiberglass "Babies." The babies weighed between two and three hundred pounds, were eleven feet long, nine feet tall and looked like monstrous wild boars raised on chemicals in the hillbilly coves of East Tennessee. Clinging to the wall of a nearby hotel was a tenth baby, an escapee from the gritty playpen. A barcode disfigured the physiognomy of each baby, the point being that calculating dehumanized. Attached to a wall overlooking the babies was a sign preaching, "so let's not get paralyzed shaming and blaming but instead learn, grow, and move on." "Huh," Vicki said, and we moved on.

Downtown Palm Springs was familiar, resembling Fort Lauderdale's Las Olas and crowded with shoppers like the androgynous tourist ports of the Caribbean. Shops sold vintage clothing and furniture, kitschy "antiques," hats, carnival costumes, crystals and wine, jewelry, sunglasses, chocolate, and cigars—complete offerings of the tacky and inessential. Here was a coffee shop; there a dispensary; above the walkway a hotel. Some stores hawked real estate, others women's clothes. Chain eateries were familiar, Starbucks and Blaze among others. Even individual restaurants with sidewalk dining were recognizable. As haberdashers sold "preloved" clothing, so menus listed foods which I had eaten in distant elsewheres and thus almost seemed "predigested." Only on the last evening when the family needed to pack and not be inconvenienced by chauffeuring did Vicki and I stray from Old Ranch and eat on Palm Canyon Drive. On the upstairs patio of Bongo Johnny's we shed our vegan radicles, drank pilsners, and ate the biggest hamburgers on the menu—medium rare, the preference of middle class carnivores.

The only store in which I spent time was Mehdi Fine Art. Some of the landscapes for sale appealed to me. Moreover, the owner was Iranian. I have long wanted to travel to and through Persia. This past fall I attempted to convince the Fulbright Scholar Program to send me to Iran as a visiting scholar. I wrote I'd be an appreciative ambassador and create good will unlike governmental policy. As could be expected, my argument didn't succeed. Perhaps I shouldn't have called the United States "a failed state." "On the high road to Hell and to becoming a failed state" would have been more tactful. Perhaps I should have refrained from referring to the wreckage wrought by American military adventurism as "the mark of the beast." For me disappointment was probably healthier than success. People are islands, and if they join the main, they oftentimes become corporate, and losing their individuality, market their integrity. Be that as it may however, the owner of the gallery planned to visit Iran in the spring and suggested I ponder accompanying him. Writing the Fulbright Program was in character but out of age. I am too old for lengthy travel, even for dreaming about the faraway, and spring will find me in Storrs planting coneflowers, the exoticism of their turbaned centers the closest I will get to the Golestan Palace, Blue Mosque, Shahzadeh Garden, and the Mausoleum of Cyrus the Great.

Along Palm Canyon Drive, embolisms of tourist families swelled and bursting out of doors, spilled children across sidewalks. So far as I could tell, locals were leashed to dogs not children. In fact dogs outnumbered children, this to be expected in a town Raymond Chandler dubbed "Poodle Springs." A man pulled a wagon loaded with pugs, and a woman holding a pink umbrella over her head even though the day was neither rainy nor sunny led a short-legged bouncing ball of white yarn. "I named her Sputnik," another man told me. "Because she was so little, I thought she needed a special name." "He's not much to look at," a man said of a graying retriever, "but he is my closest friend and I think he's beautiful." Amid the swirl of dogs and dog talk, I became separated from the family. They disappeared into a shop, and although I paced for an hour I did not find them so I returned to the hotel. I lose words when I am tired but not my sense of direction. I couldn't remember the name Old Ranch. I wondered if the hotel were the Red Rock or Rio Grande Inn. I worried that I'd be forced to ask the way and not be able to remember the hotel's name, but then I turned a corner, practically unconsciously, and found myself at the Inn.

On South Palm Canyon drive about twice as far from the Inn as the Art Museum was Moorten Botanical Garden specializing in desert plants especially cactuses. In Redwood City, Eliza has more than one hundred and twenty pots of cactuses, and one morning Eliza took us to the botanical garden. The plants were more eccentrically dressed and less prickly and irritating than people. Mother's father was a noted flower man. I inherited his green inclinations. Whenever the spine of a cactus pierces my epidermis, my vascular bundles bleed water, not blood, or so I imagine when I am in a flowering mood. Despite living in Connecticut, I was at home in the garden and recognized several plants, organ pipe, braided cholla bumpy with "Brussel sprouts," and several varieties of prickly pear, the edges of the largest thick with purple vase-shaped fruits.

Rain fell the previous night, and sparrows gathered and sipped water from the long trough-like leaves of blue agave. Golden barrel cactuses covered a slope appearing toppled like a mound of melons, the yellow haze of spines covering them giving them a sharp, not a honey dew, bite. The swollen stems of caudiciforms looked like misshapen feet, the stuff of advertisements for carnival television shows featuring foot surgery. Mammillaria senilis were the size of softballs. The white spikes laced around them made them appear youthful and vibrant, not old. I recognized desert ironwood and its smallish blue-green leaves and tecoma hung with yellow bells tinged with orange. Although grown as a house plant in spite of its scrapers of thorns, I don't think I'd seen a Madagascar Palm. Certainly with its off white trunk and long twigs of rasping thorns pushing out from wound-like holes, the boojum tree was a foreign creature. In the garden itself I heard English so rarely it, too, seemed foreign. Perhaps that was good. A wag posted a sign near a jumping cholla advising visitors to keep their distance. "Stay away," a woman said grabbing her friend's arm. "Don't you see the warning?" "Do the spikes really jump at people?" her companion asked. "Yes," the woman said pulling her friend away. "If they didn't jump, the sign wouldn't be there."

The garden was only an acre and thronged with tourists trying to control children rushing about to impale themselves. Nevertheless, for me it was a silent place, the quiet not even broken by the shriek of a child who succeeded in skewering his hand. I have lived forty-five years in a quiet corner of New England, and often the turmoil I initially thought fecund and joyful with possibilities now seems smothering. The family took two drives during Christmas, one north to Joshua Tree National Park, the other south to the Living Desert Zoo. The wasteland or indeed the desert that man has made of the desert appalled me. Once upon a time oddities attracted me, say, beside a two-lane highway, a store in a side of which was embedded a tail end of an airline fuselage and on the front porch an impossibly tall mothy bear standing on his hind legs, his paws spread in a threatening welcome. Along the highways outside Palm Springs, the tacky was every day and oddities were machine, and probably China, made. Gangs of felonious cowboys beckoned shoppers, and more dinosaurs roamed the landscape than they did in the Mesozoic era. Strip malls evolved and hatched more strip malls. South of Palm Springs cars swarmed the road and parked in hives. Next to the office of a dentist, an undertaker promoted a crematorium, and a massage therapist advertised her digital skills. "I'd rather be in Gehenna with my back broken and brain-eating amoebas mating in my molars than live near this road," I thought.

Hikes took away the winter chill and brightening days awakened the spiritual. Not soiled by the immediate detritus of the secular, desert landscapes encourage curiosity and thought. People have long recognized that places that initially appear barren are often repositories of endless riches. As winds of imagination sweep over them, dry bones suddenly live as they did for the founders of the great desert religions. Looking past the near into the distant, the begetters dreamed and created. Although our hikes did not sanctify like anointing oil, they made us feel better about ourselves, others, and our little world. As we walked water metaphorically flowed from stones. The longest walk we took in Joshua Tree National Park was three miles, composed mostly of Split Rock Loop. At the trail head we shared our lunch with a scurry of white-tailed antelope squirrels. In all the hikes I leaned on, not a wing, but ski poles and prayer. My right knee has weakened. Stepping up was usually easy; however, stepping down was difficult. My leg could not support me and would have buckled had I not had the poles. Still, I lagged, and when the others paused while I caught up, they must have longed for a closer walk with a more vigorous me.

All ages are their best apologists. Because a youthful I would have walked faster, I would have seen and appreciated less. The trail wound between mazes of granite domes and piles of boulders. Once magna the rocks were initially sculpted underground millions of years before comprehendible Time began. A ridge resembled a railway train complete with steam engine and caboose. Huge stones looked like eggs laid before the age of dinosaurs in pre- time when creatures were really large. Formations rose into buds and flowers. Water eroded the side of rocks carving love seats. A wedding cake loomed over a wash. Only one's capacity to imagine limited the formations. Beside the rocks I felt negligible and negligibly small. The feeling was comforting. How nice to be aware that not simply one's errors but that one himself does not matter. How fine to escape ego and the endless posturing depicted on radio and television. We walked beside hills of stones and across sandy flats. While we walked, the colors changed, at one moment the rocks and sand tan and washed-out blond, the next orange and red, then gray and shadowy blue.

Because I wasn't surefooted, I studied the ground more than I did the horizon. I lack the vision of a paladin, and acting as I have done since the almond tree began to flourish, I thought about the imminent and not the distant. In woods and pastures, on seashores, and in other deserts, the concrete has always attracted me more than the abstract. Keats was only partly right when he wrote, "Heard melodies are sweet, but those unheard are sweeter still." In a garden, actual fragrances are sweeter than the imaginary. As Capability Brown should have put it, a gardenia in the hand is worth two or three in a thicket over the hill. For me Joshua Tree was richer than the great English parks Brown designed.

The landscape was unfamiliar, and I identified only enough plants to make me long to see more. Here a smoke tree; over there a pinyon pine gnarly and crippled. With spines on the margins, leaves of Muller's oak resembled those of holly. Trunks of juniper were twisted and looked like a naughty boy had wrung them into what in school days were called Indian burns. Rabbit bush grew in seams between boulders while needlegrass clumped under foot. I recognized box-thorn, creosote bush, and jojoba. In the sunlight the stems of silver cholla cactuses were golden and glowed like mounds of deer antlers covered with velvet. Hedgehog cactuses huddled together looking human and unsure of themselves. Mojave yucca sprang from the ground in sprays of green daggers. More impressive was its big relative, the park's name sake, the Joshua Tree, the trunk of which broke into limbs from the ends of which leaves erupted, in daylight looking electrified, at night bewitched.

At the end of the walk, I wished I'd explored Joshua Tree when my legs were elastic with the verve of middle age. But that feeling passed quickly. This was Christmas, a time for celebrating doing, not lamenting the undone or the impossible to do. The hike was a dandy gift, and unwrapping it made me long for the other walks Eliza and Travis planned. Twice in the following days we drove to Indian Canyons and took short hikes, one on the Loop Trail in Andreas Canyon, the longer three miles along Palm Canyon and Victor trails. Beside the trails grew California fan palms. Dead brown leaves clung to the trunks of the palms looking like shaggy petticoats or great grass skirts worn by mythological dancers to welcome visitors. Atop the trees crowns of green leaves splayed open like accordions and in the quiet away from the jabber of families played lively silent polkas. Hanging on the trees were bunches of ripe grape-sized black fruits. When they fall to the ground, mammals eat them. They digest the outer flesh but not the hard inner seeds and along the trails were small mounds of coyote scat bumpy with rust-colored seeds.

Droppings open doors into the life at one's feet— the actual places in which people live unlike conjectural worlds beyond the clouds. For decades I have rummaged through droppings. On the trails were small piles of fur voided by coyotes or foxes. Although the piles looked like remnants of mice or wood rats, they were not bony and strangely exuded a tincture of fish. Unfortunately since the virus caught me in February, my sense of smell has been unreliable. The aromas of animal feces have been especially arbitrary. Road apples don't smell like Winesaps or Macouns, but neither do their fragrances bring barns and pastures to mind. As could be expected, in Indian Canyons I sagged behind my family. Once when I rested on the lip of a calloused ridge examining a handful of fur, a robustly conventional couple approached and asked what I was doing. I showed them the fur and offered them a complimentary sniff. They declined and hurried away. Shortly afterward, they met Eliza and Vicki who were waiting for me. "Be careful," they warned, "there is a crazy man on the trail. He's not far behind and will try to sell you excrement." Again, my Southern accent led to a misunderstanding and doused color over a drab conversation. Sometimes when people hear me, preconceived notions affect their comprehension and obscure the words spoken. Often the mistakes startle but rarely do they irritate. How nice for a gimpy retired college teacher to be thought a feces salesman. "The best in the Southwest," I told Eliza. "Unlike veterinarians who specialize in the excretory processes of either big or small animals, I am a general cloacalist."

Amid the fan palms shimmered copses of Fremont cottonwoods. In sunlight their leaves flowed like droplets of yellow honey. Along low creeks stood western sycamores. Their trunks were so white and straight they looked planed and bleached. For much of the time we hiked the canyons, the sky was uninviting, and the single unfamiliar bird I spied was a loggerhead shrike. Gathered along the edges of Palm Canyon Trail were dumps of fronds, fruit stalks, and trunks. I assumed the piles sheltered assorted small creatures, among others rats and snakes, lizards and frogs. I hoped to but did not see a California kingsnake. It would have been a good addition to my reptile record, the ophidian watcher's equivalent of a birder's list. Black and ringed by white bands, the snake can live for two decades, grow to four feet, and is an omnivore feeding on a buffet of creatures including other snakes. As the trees themselves were potential firebrands so the piles were flammable hazards. However boring beetles killed more trees than flames. Fires charred the trunks and burned the skirts wrapping fan palms. However, because much of the palms' vascular tissue lay deep within their trunks and not near the outer bark, the trees survived fires and quickly produced new Kelley green crowns.

The day before Vicki and I flew back to Connecticut. Eliza drove to the ticket office of the Aerial Tramway at seven in the morning and bought tickets for the nine o'clock tram. The tram travelled two and a half miles up from Coachella Valley along the hard, gullied sides of Chino Canyon. It took ten minutes to reach the mountain terminal in San Jacinto Park, 8,516 feet above sea level. A snow fell the night before, and when we reached the station, wind banged so strongly that when people stepped out of the station building onto the terrace it spun and bent them. The snow transformed the gradual paved path from the station down to the mountain forest into an icy goat way. At the foot of the path, the forest blocked and shuffled the wind, but Vicki and I had not brought boots to Palm Springs and the snow made hiking any strand of the web of high trails too difficult. I prefer flood-plain valleys to rugged heights, but the great pines warmed our moment in the park: Jeffrey pines that many people claim smell like butterscotch, an aroma which I could not detect, then great ponderosa pines, their bark rough plates looking like cuirasses dented, holed, and russet from age.

That afternoon we drove to the Living Desert Zoo and Gardens, a traffic-plagued trip from downtown Palm Springs. The zoo was located on the edge of the Santa Rosa Hills on gritty unspoiled roughage between golf clubs and beyond housing developments where UPS and Fed Ex trucks ranged freely. Although rich with desert plant communities, the gardens were deserted, that is, by visitors, all of whom including us had come to see animals. Zoos both intrigue and depress me. While the variety of creatures simultaneously invigorates appreciation for the richness of life, it also makes me lament man's inhumanity to the inhuman. "Stone walls do not a prison make, / Nor iron bars a cage," Richard Lovelace wrote in the seventeenth century. But, of course, walls do make prisons and bars, cages. How terrible to see a single kookaburra in a small cage, a bird whose wild laughter shatters spleen and listeners' confining moods. How sad to watch a caracal endlessly pacing, a sight that does not make a person cherish beautiful multiplicity but instead evokes grim cognizance of the repetitive nature of his own life restricted to asphalt paths and paved behavior. Reptile houses are almost always inadequate. Bull snakes can grow to eight feet and should not be confined to barren utilitarian glass cages but should be free to roam. Wondrously blotched yellow, blue-black, and red, they should be sudden aesthetic discoveries. A man in the reptile house told me that he thought "goodbye by snake preferable to goodbye by morphine." At the time he was looking at a red diamond rattlesnake. The snake was beautiful, but it was mildly venomous and its bite only would finish people already falling off their last legs.

The enclosure for big horned sheep was large and happily adequate. It reached into the rocky low hills along one side of the zoo and allowed the sheep to climb and perch. Generally, the animals that caught my eye now were not those that attracted me when I was young, that is, creatures commonly celebrated as elegant and lovely like giraffes or cute like addra gazelles. Instead I was typically drawn to "homely" birds like the Kori bustard, its body a fin or aileron atop long legs, and the northern ground hornbill, the blue circle around each of its eyes larger than those on Pete the Pup. Moreover, in the zoo I liked the heavy mothy and mildewed aroma of Chacoan peccaries. "Insectariums are my favorite parts of zoos," a man said to me, adding that the world's best were in the Far East. I have been in only a couple of insectariums, but I think I agree with the man.

Occupying three-fourths of an acre in the middle of the zoo was the Bighorn Railway featuring G-scale model trains and 3200 feet of track. Trains ran through towns and across bridges and high trestles. They passed logging and mining camps, the Grand Canyon, and the Rocky Mountains. Instead of boarding a train and riding the rails, I studied model buildings, but rather than appreciating the whole, I jotted down a single insignificant observation. Painted over the door of a purple house was "Kitty Rescue." Looking out the windows of the house and lounging about the yard were fourteen toy cats. At times I stopped walking and my mind drifted. By the entrance to the zoo, a shop sold stuffed animals. I wondered if owning a menagerie of stuffed animals increased or decreased the attraction of live animals to children. "Emma, listen to me. You are all done, all done," a weary mother shouted at a small girl rattling a fence in hopes of frightening a pair of ostriches.

"Zoos make me melancholy," Vicki said that night. "I prefer places like Joshua Tree where the lives of animals are private rather than public, where a sense of freedom exists even if it is an illusion." The next morning Travis took us to the airport. We flew to Dallas where we had a three-hour layover, after which we changed planes and flew on to Hartford. We landed at mid-night, fetched the car at Lazfly, and drove home, getting in at one-thirty. Christmas was over, and I decided I had taken my last long flight. My left leg shook uncontrollably from Dallas to Hartford, and during the initial day at home my feet were big as cantaloupes. That first night we slept six hours then drove to Pomfret to pick up the dogs before the kennel closed. After dinner that evening Vicki was so tired, she forgot to put the dogs out, and Suzie had an accident in the living room. "Nothing has changed," Vicki said as she doused the floor with Nature's Miracle.

Vicki was right. Life was the same. During the day two robocallers telephoned, one from Miami, the other from Oxford, Maryland, and a "functionary" from Amazon sent an email. He informed me that my $599 purchase had been mailed. He added that if the charge was incorrect, I should contact him immediately, so he could cancel the shipment and refund the payment to my charge card, the number of which he needed to verify. Inflation really is rampant. The last time a crook wrote me and identified himself as an Amazon employee my purchase was $499. In another email, Tchao Ago Bazaa notified me that one of his clients recently died intestate. The man's last name was the same as mine. I assume Tchao refrained from citing Pickering in the correspondence for security reasons. Delegated, however, to unearth heirs, he urged family members to "come forward," instructing them to reply to his email and provide their "full names" and their "Private Telephone Number."

Our first day was full. Before lunch I cancelled a three-week Caribbean cruise on Holland America scheduled for February. I cancelled everything: the cruise, flights to Fort Lauderdale, hotels, and a parking reservation. I did so because I worried that Vicki and I would fly to Florida, get tested for Omicron, be found positive, and be marooned at Port Everglades, left behind like Ben Gunn when *The Walrus* sailed. That afternoon Eric delivered our mail, and I opened Christmas cards. "May your season be bright," my "Volvo Family" wrote despite my not having driven a Volvo in four years. On the card sent by Retirement Security stood a grove of five trees decorated with shiny red Christmas ornaments. Branches of the trees were laden with snow, but I could tell they were spruces not pines. In her card Bethany wrote that in spite of God's being "in Control," she prayed for America every day. Steve wrote that he hoped to see "the world population decline," a statement with which I agreed after navigating roads in and around Palm Springs. Above Bill's letter appeared the caption "Our Year Of Worrying About Other People Worrying About Us Having Covid." Bill and his wife Peggy are travelers and despite being vaccinated and even receiving a premature booster had been tested nine times. People my age often send photographs of grandchildren. In writing about grandchildren, they infrequently mention things other than the sports the children play. One or two sent family pictures. Depicting sixteen people, Jeffrey and Varina's was the most populous and made me happy with envy, if an envious person can be happy. My old friends were not Mormonic, however. In the picture they appeared surrounded by their three offspring and their spouses, and eight grandchildren, three boys and five girls, the youngest girl hugging a stuffed monkey.

Among the cards was a single present. Every

year a cousin so far removed she believes we are closely related sends Vicki and me a carton of petit fours. The small cakes are glazed in seductive gay colors bringing to mind, Vicki says, "childhood and the excitement of a box of new crayons." Eating a petit four iced in red inevitably leads to a bite of one wrapped in Christmas green. Next come chocolate, lemon, and in some Decembers purple cakes topped by drizzles of sprinkles. To avoid abdominal swellings and the need of medicinal trocars, Vicki and I no longer sample the petit fours. We don't leave them in the kitchen long enough to gaze on them with lust on our palates. As soon as we open the present, Vicki says, "Get thee from me Limos," dumps the cakes into the sink, turns on the water and the garbage disposal, and we have a "Churnfest." Immediately thereafter, I write a thank-you note fulsome with praise. This year I said that although the petit fours were scrumptious and deliciously sweet, the thought behind them was sweeter. They were "love on a plate" warming our return from zephyrous California to frosty Connecticut. "Aren't you ashamed?" Vicki said after scanning the note. I wasn't. I've grown comfortable with my limitations. Literary hypocrisy does not discommode me. Besides, when tired I often thrust my pen into the hand of a half-remembered character from an addlepated novel and delegate the writing to him. Sometimes he giggles. Sometimes he brays, but no matter how disconcerting the sounds, he manages the chore.

Despite being so busy or maybe because of it, I could not fall asleep that night, so I started reading George Barr McCutcheon's *The Man from Brodneys*, published in 1908, the novel like most of McCutcheon's books is a natural soporific. McCutcheon's characters and their courtships are cozily familiar. Adventures pitched at high keys never rise above low notes, and instead of bounding forward creating tension, the stories saunter, allowing, practically encouraging, readers to drift away and return at will, to call narrative time outs. As a result, finishing a volume is a lackadaisical process always lasting more than a week. Hollingsworth Chase, the hero and the man from Brodneys, was particularly and personally appealing, guaranteeing that I'd read slowly and carelessly. He and Sam Pickering had little in common, but he and The Truth were cut from the same roustabout rags.

After graduating from Yale law school and wasting two years clerking for a judge and living a hopelessly respectable life, Chase decamped and headed to Turkestan. During the following years, he spent time as a war correspondent for "a great newspaper." He acted as agent for hemp dealers in the Philippines, hunted in Asia and Africa, "carried a rifle with the Boers in South Africa," took forbidden photographs in St. Petersburg, and on an expedition "almost got to the North Pole." "To do and be all of these," McCutcheon judged, "he had to be a manly man." Not in a month's journey would anyone [who did not know The Truth] meet "a truer thoroughbred, a more agreeable chap, a more polished vagabond." "First lieutenant in Dame Fortune's army," he was tall, good looking, rawboned, cheerful, and gallant, "the true comrade of those merry, reckless volunteers from all lands who find commissions in Fortune's army and serve her faithfully." If his and The Truth's paths had crossed and merged, only the limitations of the reader's imagination could have curtailed the adventures of the pair. In any case despite not meeting his doppelganger, Chase lived expansively, sharing "pot luck in odd parts of the world with English lords, German barons and French counts." Although not in The Truth's league, he was an amorist. "His heart," McCutcheon gossiped, "had withstood the importunate batterings of many a love siege; the wounds had been pleasant ones and the recovery quick. He left no dead behind him."

After falling asleep while following Chase's antics, visions of Bekmes and Nabat danced in my head. That afternoon the wind squalled, and a heavy snow fell. By dusk the temperature was in the single digits. Before teatime I raised one of the garage doors four feet off the ground so that birds could fly inside and spend the night sheltered from the wind. Before going to bed I shut the door. The next morning, I got up early and opened it. Two wrens flew out, and I shoveled the driveway. Vicki worries that I will keel over. Sam Pickering's heart is wonky, and he might collapse. But The Truth is made of softer, more endurable arteries. In the afternoon a red fox appeared near the den in the back yard. Unless an automobile intervenes, kits will surface in the spring. Vicki and I will argue about my supplementing their diet with dog food. Vicki says doing so is unnatural. She is right, but feeding them makes me feel part of nature, and I will feed them. The vixen and her kits are the brightest flowers of my spring. They turn the barren yard into a garden, and I love watching them bloom. If Vicki's criticism becomes shrill, I will behave like Sam Pickering, moan, and clutch my chest.

January 28, 2022: There won't be any kits in the spring.

# Suicide by Pen

Books have short lives. No matter that people talk about a volume for ten, twenty or even a hundred years, it will vanish into the silence of the stillborn. Words disappear, and although an occasional author imagines writing himself into perpetuity, immortality by pen does not exist. On the other hand, suicide by pen is epidemic. Hordes of authors continue to write after being forgotten. "The dose makes the poison," and the toxins from the increasing accumulation of pages seeps into their reputations and eventually consigns their better books to the de-activation skip. Even when suffering from the feverish daydream of posthumous acclaim, writers don't expect librarians to explore the stacks, discover a treasure chest of their books, and carrying it to the circulation desk, save the volumes from drowning in dust. Authors write not because books matter, but because writing is what they do. Although they realize "The End" is nonfiction, they'd rather treat it as fiction.

On the inside pockets on the left side of the sport coats I wore fifty years ago are tell-tale blue stains. Dry cleaning and attic years have obscured the blotches, but traces remain visible without the aid of luminol. Happily, no longer do pens drip like faucets, and felo-de-se by pen is now comparatively neat and easy on the eye. However, for some writers suicide by pen is too slow. Rather than endure the gradual decline of their pages, they prefer to take leave of their writing lives swiftly. A librarian friend did that last year although I think his demise accidental rather than intentional. He was overweight, seventy-six years old, a bachelor, and a drinker. Four years earlier he had heart surgery. Afterward his cardiologist urged him to monitor his eating, a prescription which my friend duly ignored. The day he finished his "great book," he bought a double magnum of Champagne, an assortment of soft cheeses, among others, Brie, Camembert, and his favorite St. Andre, and then a bakery of loaves, sourdough, artisan, and ciabatta. Once he gathered the provisions, he settled down for a celebratory night of eating. It was his last supper. Before the sun rose and before he felt obliged to ponder a new topic, he had a stroke.

What led a few people to suspect suicide by mouth was that his funeral instructions were detailed. Not only did he prepay the cost of his cremation but before he began the conclusion of his study he commissioned a personalized receptacle for his ashes: a wooden container shaped like a folio. Carved on the lid was the title of his magnum opus, "A Bibliography of the Works of Harold MacGrath: His Novels, Short Stories, and Films." On the next line appeared "By" followed by my friend's name, under which appeared the years of his birth and death. MacGrath was popular and prolific. From 1900 through 1930, he turned out at least fifty volumes, many of which became films. My friend spent untold years compiling the bibliography. It was a labor of fetish, not one reciprocated by others. Today MacGrath is an absence not a presence. To provide matter for conversation with my friend I read two of MacGrath's novels, *A Splendid Hazard* and *The Man on the Box*. I read them before I contemplated suicide by pen. They are, however, books which a person intent on paring the size of his audience should recommend to readers.

In the past I took notes when I read. From MacGrath's volumes I jotted down a single quotation, this from *The Man on the Box*. Elizabethan poets often described the faces of women in extravagant terms, comparing teeth to pearls, lips to cherries, skin to ivory, and eyes to precious jewels. Only once have I read mention of a woman's nostrils. This occurred in a parody in which the "poet" compared his beloved's nares to avocados. In *The Box* the narrator noted that as Betty Annesley leaned against a railing on an ocean liner her chin was tilted. The angle enabled "Warburton," her husband to be after three hundred and fifty pages, to "tell by the dilated nostrils that she was breathing in the gale with all the joy of living, filling her healthy lungs with it as that rare daughter of the Cyprian Isle [Venus] might have done as she sprang that morn from the jeweled Mediterranean." At the time I thought the narrator had fallen into silly poetic seas. "The poor girl," I told Vicki, "will probably suffer from a terrible sinus infection. Think how she will snort and hack." Recently I changed my mind. MacGrath's novel was published in 1904 when tuberculosis cut down gardens of beauteous girls before they bloomed. Betty's alveoli were healthy, and she was the hardy budding stuff of matrimony.

Groups as well as individuals commit suicide by pen. Many academic books are swamps in which a rational person dare not dip his eye. This is especially true of the humanities in which some departments, often English, have long entertained death wishes. Out of the ashes of incoherence, practitioners expect fresher studies will rise like the Phoenix, hot stuff, its wings red and golden with generative sunlight, its feathers beating and creating more culturally relevant disciplines. On occasion a person simply mutters "to Hell with it all" and purposely writes something that will dynamite his career and blacken his reputation. Unfortunately, the effects of meticulous planning are often unexpected. Social conjunctivitis is common, and the eyes of beholders blink and blear. What one reader thinks a smothering cloud of soot, another believes is the inspirational comet-like trail of a Roman candle.

Moreover, recollection is capricious. People swiftly forget whether publicity is bad or good. If they recall it at all, they remember it as only publicity, not so much damning as drawing attention to something ponderable. Recently a university in Alabama remarkable only for being undistinguished and unremarked cancelled a talk by a Pulitzer prize-winning heuristic public intellectual. The school scrapped the talk because the man supported Planned Parenthood. As a result, the school garnered more publicity than it received during the past twenty years. Whether the attention was favorable or unfavorable didn't matter; it put the university "on the map" almost as successfully as a championship athletic team and at much less expense.

Suicide by pen sometimes fails or at least pauses. Like a defibrillator an old concern occasionally rejuvenates a dying interest or like a shot of adrenaline the unexpected shocks the comatose writer, breaking his sleep and causing his pen to drip ink. However, great or not so great awakenings occur more often in churches than in studies. Generally, writers fade away premortem. The older a writer the less vigorous he becomes and the smaller the chance of his stumbling across an enlivening new subject. Instead, he gathers fragments and oddities for "future use." "That reflects life," Josh said. "Days are piecemeal affairs." Last year, Josh continued, "I read a remark by a man who said he slept a great deal because he didn't approve of being idle. Shortly afterward in Clifford Conner's *A People's History of Science*, I learned that Jakob Nufer who castrated farm animals for a living in Switzerland 'performed the first recorded caesarian section on a live mother in about 1500.'" The operation succeeded. The baby and mother survived, and supposedly the mother bore more children and lived until she was seventy-seven. Josh said the statement and the fact belonged in a graveyard of paragraph parts, here a carburetor and a direct object, there a noun clause and a radiator. "If a writer uses all the parts in the yard at once, his pages won't turn over. But a selective few are good inertia starter motors," Josh declared then concluded, saying "fragments are what we are and fragments are all we have. And to quote the old Polish proverb, the observant man looks at the woodpile and sees the forest."

Josh can be too professorial. "Uuuggghhhh," as Ray Wylie Hubbard sang in "Snake Farm," the "reptile house" where Ramona the narrator's girlfriend worked. "The history of the humblest human is a tale of marvels," Samuel Smiles stated in the preface to his life of Thomas Edward, "A Scotch Naturalist." Maybe, but maybe not. On Ramona's arm was a tattoo of a python eating a little mouse. On its head the python wore a sailor hat saying, "Snake Farm." Still, as I have endured beyond my allotted time, I think in scraps and live scrappily. Marvels don't punctuate my days, and my life resembles a collection of idiosyncratic anecdotes, not a genre as elevated as a tale. Yet the life is mine, and it satisfies me. Yesterday Vicki and

I and our packlet of rescue dogs walked through the wood above the Fenton River. I have lost my sense of balance, and when we crossed streams, I avoided steppingstones and walked through the water. "Old age and the goddamn medicines I take have done this to me," I complained to Vicki. "Sam," she said, "mind your language in front of the dogs."

Our dog Suzie is sixteen years old, deaf, and almost blind. Throughout the day she whimpers. In the house she wanders aimlessly, gets underfoot, and begs to go outside every hour. On a walk she must be leashed. If not, she becomes confused, turns around, and runs back along the way we came. Because she is deaf, she cannot hear us shouting. Although her mind is pocked, she is physically strong and outruns us when we chase her. Our "good dog" has become a nuisance, so much so that the reservoir of affection that the shared years built up has leached away, drying Vicki's and my conversation about her. As we sat on a slope above a beaver lodge, Vicki looked at Suzie and asked, "Do you think she is in pain," the question prelude to justifying an act that would ease our lives.

Suzie has always been my girl, and I crinkled that scrap of thought and tossed it out of mind for the moment. Soon another scrap floated across my path. Once Vicki and I talked to a man gathering mushrooms, but the only people we see regularly in the woods are fellow dog walkers and then the occasional undergraduate couple, the two not lovers but that better duo boyfriend and girlfriend. We relax and amble. "When I was a boy roaming in Tennessee and Virginia, I couldn't shed the fear that someone was watching me," I said to Vicki. "No matter the surface calm, in the South there is always an undertow of potential violence. That's not so in New England." "Rubbish,"

Vicki said. "You've read too much Faulkner, and probably too much Thoreau. Think about a different topic. How about raking leaves? You must do that when we get home." I'd already scraped the yard bare three times and at least one more round lay ahead of me. Oddly, when I blow, rake, and cart leaves, I don't think about anything. The work strains my muscles but rests my mind. The next morning, I am mentally refreshed and ready for the next signpost marking the way toward "The End."

The ostensibly endless "leafing" is probably a metaphor, but I haven't decided what it means. Many fragments that collect in the minds of writers slowly committing suicide by pen are familiar. They are more repetitive than fall and summertime chores. Every day in high school I had a math test. After graduation the tests did not abandon me and have accompanied me all my life. At least once every two months I dream that I am walking into math class unprepared for the daily test. I don't fail the tests because I always wake up sweaty but relieved. The most recent time the dream roused me was last Friday. I went downstairs, sat at the kitchen table, and drank a glass of orange juice. "The real effect of education," I muttered then suddenly thought of another effect. For four years in high school, I wrote a theme every fortnight. I turned the theme in on Friday accompanied by two rough drafts and two outlines. "No wonder I'm committing suicide by pen. The lead got into my bloodstream. No diuretic will purge it and stop my writing themes, the only difference being that I now call them articles."

As writers age their worlds become less clamorous. For many the addiction to attention subsides so much they become consciously reclusive, and Josh says, "delude themselves into believing that they are not committing suicide by pen but have retired from the public eye in order to focus on writing final masterpieces, books that will attract readers other than fans of obituary pages." Oatmeal colored hands are not as strong as those that gleam like baby oil, and they write less in order to marshal their strength. Amid the jittery chatter of living, bombast like that of Josh quickly loses force. Explanations fade, but no matter how retiring one becomes oddities will dip across his sight and settle in his mind like leaves on the ground. My body parts are in the shop so often that concocting an acceptable excuse for begging off things social is easy. I simply convey regrets and say, "alas," or "woe is me, I have a doctor's appointment." I use the excuse repeatedly because I turn down all invitations. So far no one has doubted my sincerity. "Of course, not," Vicki said, "how many people would respond by exclaiming, 'bullshit, haven't you had enough treatments for cancer?'" I don't know such people, but I wouldn't mind meeting one or two. They'd be good copy, outspoken like the acquaintance who advised me not to shake hands with a political calumniator. "To throw dung, a person has to scoop it up. Nubbins stick to his palms and lodge under his fingernails. As a result he soils whatever he touches."

Recently old schoolmates planned a reunion for people who graduated sixty-six years ago from Parmer elementary school in Nashville. In describing his euphoria at the beginning of the French Revolution, Wordsworth wrote, "Bliss was it in that dawn to be alive. But to be young was very heaven!" To grow up in Nashville and attend Parmer were for me greater bliss. Time tarnished the Revolution, but memories of my childhood shine like a sterling silver table setting, rarely seen but always glimpsed on holidays. I remember the years uncritically, and my affection for those children, my young, now old, school friends runs deeper than love. I wish them well. But I won't attend the reunion. I don't want the stridency of my Now or that of theirs to stain memories. I suppose the hesitancy to attend reflects the cowardice of age, my fear of being so tottery I won't cross a stream on steppingstones, much less embrace the touchstones of my past. When the reunion occurs, I'll be at home. I will be melancholy and metaphorically die a little. But I will be occupied, at my desk early in the morning penning my way to suicide, gathering fragments of life, trying to piece them together before the sun sets.

No one knows himself well enough to be certain about the reasons he does or does not do many things. Earlier this year in a dream I walked through an art gallery. Oil paintings hung on the walls of every room. Instead of looking at the canvases, I studied the frames surrounding them and then only a small section of each frame, the lower left corner. Occasionally I passed an oval mirror. I didn't notice the glass. Instead, I looked at the arc where the left corner would have been had the frame not been circular. I doubt the dream reveals anything about me. Still, parts, or little things, satisfy me. I'm not a "whole picture" person. One spring years ago I demurred when a literary maker invited me to be his guest at a dinner in New York. Vicki's and my children were young. In the fall they helped me plant hundreds of daffodils in the dell outside my study. "Thank you for the invitation," I wrote, "but at the time of the dinner daffodils will be blooming, and I can't miss gathering bouquets with the children. They've already told me they want to give them to their mother. What happiness!" Perhaps the inevitable narrowing of life that accompanies age does not upset me because frames content me. Maybe that's the reason "suicide by pen" appeals to me. Rather than foreshadowing loss, it continues the life I enjoy. The days when my writing flowered are over, but wilt is compensation enough. Besides, with care, and luck, my pages might make a swell potpourri.

Sometimes I imagine the progress of suicide by pen looking like a snake that has swallowed a nest of baby birds. The snake is torpid and moves slowly, the little birds lumps in its stomach. Practically every day is lumpy with something. On Wednesday the cable box for the television stopped working. That evening a technician exchanged it for another box. The cable company doesn't scrap broken boxes. It repairs them, erases their contents, and packs then back out as replacements. The person who repaired our "new" box neglected to erase programs recorded by the previous user. Clearly the family had children as they recorded forty-six programs from the Disney Channel. Also on the box were nine episodes of "Rosanne," "not indicative of PBS taste," Vicki said. In the rebuilder's oversight lay the seeds of story. From shows forgotten in a cable box, a quick writer could spin a web of tales. The effort didn't appeal to me, and like a sidewinder I moved laterally and opened George Barr McCutcheon's *Castle Craneycrow*. Spending hours hunting the world's flaws causes the griping colic. McCutcheon's novels don't make intellectual or emotional demands. Neither do they sweep readers out of comfortable placidity. They are dated, often poorly written, and so dull little can be said about them making them suitable reading for a writer contemplating suicide by pen. Unless deluded by a religious mythology, the aged are pessimists. Unlike the optimist who frequently devolves into a man of misguided action, the pessimist is a man of inaction, the right lethargic reader for McCutcheon's novels.

I chose the book because of the title, not its contents or reputation. In the early nineteenth century Craney Crow appeared in a counting out rhyme. Later, the rhyme became a song. Spellings aside, McCutcheon's version was traditional, "Chick o' me, Chick o' me, Craneycrow, / Went to the well to wash her toe, / When she got back her chicken was dead— / Chick o' me, Chick o' me, chop off his head— / What time is it, old witch?" Selecting a title from children's verse suited the story. At times the tale was infantile, making the book easy for a reader to count out for a while and attend to other things. I stopped reading to answer a telephone call from Bliss Boutique, a consignment shop in Willimantic. A clerk told me she mailed Vicki a check for $28.60 for clothes "dropped off" the previous week. One morning Andre arrived from Thomas Electric to service the generator. At CVS I got a coronavirus booster shot. The next day I felt so bad I couldn't read. On Saturday we ate lunch at Aero Diner in Windham across Route 6 from "The Country Club," known to the uninitiated as Walmart. Afterward we visited the club. While Vicki bought hand cream and animal crackers, I roamed the store. I counted sixteen people puttering about on motorized shopping carts. Near the cash register on aisle four, I found a dime. On the sidewalk outside the entrance a little girl told me her puppy was named Zuko, and in the parking lot, I grabbed Vicki's elbow and steered her away from a wad of chewing gum on the ground. "You have always been an invaluable guide," Vicki said.

Craneycrow castle had bastions and parapets and was "the grimmest, feudliest, ghastliest old place between Brussels and Anthony Hope's domain"—Brussels being the scene of much of the story and Hope's domain Ruritania, being a country thoroughly explored by adolescent dreamers. Snakes and bats inhabited lost tunnels, and in the castle's secret dungeon a skeleton collapsed into dust and lost its head. The plot was a farrago of fights, murders, kidnappings, love talk, and glarings, in these last the eyes of the hero scalding, those of the villain cold. A mild-mannered New Yorker shot the jaw off a Russian assassin in a duel. So many plots splotched the narrative that the main story disappeared. Among the characters was a tuft hunting American dowager intent on marrying her repressed but wealthy daughter to a foreign prince. The daughter Dorothy was a diamond in the shy and so beautiful that "no novelist" could describe her. In contrast the prince was a demon, the red blood on his hands thicker than the blue blood slithering through his veins. Quentin, the hero, was a gentleman roisterer, often thoughtless but nonetheless selfless and generous, a man about the world untainted by the world. His man servant was Turk a diminutive an ex-burglar preternaturally adept at discovering malefactors. When Quentin said Turk had eyes in the back of his head, Turk responded, "Eyes, nothin'! They is microscopes."

"It has been said," McCutcheon wrote, that "it is only the ridiculously improbable projects that are successful." After three hundred and ninety pages, a rope of plots garroted the novel. Untangling them was too much for McCutcheon, and he concluded the book by ignoring them and suddenly marrying Quentin to Dorothy. In a novel when much that could turn out badly ends in a marriage, older, less critical readers who have lived through countless disappointments often ignore absurdity and in cheery nuptial spirits smile at happy endings. For me the book succeeded because I spent three weeks reading it, averaging 19 pages a day. No aspect of the tale compelled me to read faster, and I had time for sundry chores.

On the morning I finished the novel, I tidied the yard. I gathered the last leaves falling from two small sugar maples. Yellow and red, and platter-sized, they were so beautiful they made me almost regret folding my tarpaulin and putting it and my rake into garage storage. Of course, all tidying is momentary. Although Vicki pays for almost everything with a charge card, she occasionally uses a check. Last month after noticing that only a handful of checks from the batch purchased a dozen years ago remained, she ordered a new cache. "What was I thinking?" she asked when the new checks arrived. "I ordered five hundred. If I write twenty-five checks a year, which I won't, the supply won't run low for twenty years. By then I'll be so old I'll won't be able to write and will have forgotten my name." "Don't worry," I said. "The old checks will last through this year. By next Christmas I'm sure you will use one or two of the new checks, and over time as your memory gets fuzzy, you'll misplace at least three hundred."

People intent upon literal self-murder rather than that by pen should not read *Castle Craneycrow*. The book doesn't awaken throbbing anxiety. It is a blood pressure reducer. It undermines the will and capacity to act and is a more efficacious a life-extender than Amlodipine or Benazepril. On the other hand, writers thirsting to commit suicide by pen and aching to escape the burden of admiration should recommend the book to others. Indeed, writing about it is a reputation-bender. As people age their actions become more habitual, and *unique* disappears from their lives and speech. Moreover, their hankering for the potato chips and cheese puffs on the literary table increase. Perhaps it would be more accurate to say, "under the literary table." Consequently, for my next reading I selected *The Purple Parasol* another novel by McCutcheon. I thought the book would be balmy and recuperative. Not only would it sedate readers more effectively than Xanax, but it would cap my writing career like a cover sealing a well on an abandoned farm. I chose the book because its title was the name of a mushroom. In budding writing days I once imagined a series of books with titles taken from plants, among others *Old Man of the Andes* and *Peacock Plant*. The former is a cactus covered with unkempt white hair. Hidden beneath the hair are red spikes, fitting for an eccentric middle-aged sleuth. With its glistening green leaves, their veins darker and swelling ornate across the upper surfaces like feathers, its lower, foundation, surfaces pink and purple, the Peacock Plant suited a secret agent, a glossy seductive indoor woman. "Woe be to the man who falls in love with her," I thought.

"And woe to the promising young lawyer Samuel W. Rossiter, Jr. only two years out of Yale," McCutcheon wrote in the first pages of the *Parasol*. Seventy and "a sight," the millionaire Godfrey Wharton had married "one of the prettiest, gayest, young women" in New York. While he was an "old crocodile," she was a smoochably-inclined twenty-five. Discovering money was not a warm comforter, she soon tumbled out of the marriage bed and into the arms of an actor. After the affair became talk of the town, Wharton decided to divorce his wife. Determined to do so with as little expense as possible, he hired the firm for which Rossiter worked, instructing him to amass a folder of incriminating settlement-reducing evidence. On Wharton's discovering that his wife and her paramour planned to forsake the city and snuggle together in a rural love nest in the Adirondacks, Rossiter was assigned to shadow her. Beauty and the purple parasol she carried made her easily identifiable. The novel was a light-hearted love d'esprit. Harrison Fisher illustrated the book, and the heroine was a Fisher girl. Tall and slender with flowering hair and given to wearing dresses that flowed smoother than water and never eddied, she was the Yalie's dream, a romantic type endangered in 1905 and extinct today.

On his first appearance Rossiter wore a dark gray, double-breasted suit, brown and white saddle shoes, and a straw hat. His shirt had a ruffled front topped by a starched round collar. His trousers were cuffed and fitted as they should, loose with a slight break above his shoes. His uniform smacked more of the parlor than it did of hiking or espionage, and he smoked too many cigars to be a real outdoorsman. In romantic novels identities are fragile, and an experienced reader could guess after fewer than nineteen pages that Rossiter made a mistake. He wasn't dogging the erring Mrs. Wharton but the wholesome Helen Dering. Instead of absconding from an aged spouse, she was fleeing the importuning proposals of James Dudley one of the richest men in New York. Dudley was tall, dark, handsome, decent, and owned yachts, automobiles, railways, and big mines in South America, but Helen just didn't love him.

During the course of the novel Helen came to love Rossiter who like a good spy followed her every footstep, not discovering "a very dark page" in her past but instead that he loved her. Eventually becoming disgusted with "being a sneak," he wrote his employers and resigned. They answered immediately informing him that ten days earlier the real Mrs. Wharton and her leading man had absconded to Europe. Shortly afterward Rossiter explained himself to Helen and confessed his love. "She heard him through without a word," silent because his fervor and the unexpected turn of events startled her. But then "the light in her eyes changed," McCutcheon wrote. "There grew, by stages, wonder, incredulity, wavering doubt and— joy. She understood him and she loved him!" Rossiter was flabbergasted when he learned that the man he mistook for an actor was James Dudley, "the man with the millions." "Good Lord!" he exclaimed addressing Helen, "And you could have had him instead of me? Helen, I—I don't understand it. Why didn't you take him?" Helen hesitated "a moment before answering brightly." "Perhaps," she said, "it is because I have a fancy for the ridiculous."

The next two words on the page were "THE END." But, of course, that wasn't the end. Fictional characters ignore periods, and their lives sprawl far beyond the page. Helen had the makings of a good essayist in her. If she donned her favorite sailor hat, sat at the desk in Sam's study, and raised a yellow parasol above her head, there is no telling what charming, fanciful paragraphs she might write. McCutcheon thought himself a couture. But he could have learned a trick or two about the modish from Helen. Perhaps he did. In a later novel one of his well-dressed sweethearts observed that although the "frock usually makes the woman" it doesn't always make the lady.

# Afterword

In Harold MacGrath's *A Splendid Hazard*, an adventurer down on his uppers but soon to thrive as a villain toasted success. He began with a prelude, raising his glass to "A man who knows how to drink his wine, a woman who knows when to laugh," and "a story-teller who stops when his point is told." The references to winebibbers and women are vulgar, but that to the story-teller is on the mark especially when the narrator's mark is a period. "None ever wished it longer," Dr. Johnson said of *Paradise Lost*. Few people read Milton today. Instead, they watch television, seemingly misled by the adage "a picture is worth a thousand words." Of course, a picture is simply a picture, composed of such things as symmetrical balance and the rule of thirds, but never lines of iambic pentameter. However, all people who have focused on a printed page, be it an article in a magazine, a novel, or an advertisement tacked to a notice board, have experienced the impatient hankering for brevity or "The End." I have reached the age of endings. Many of my childhood friends have taken leaves of absence from life and are experiencing, as the chaplain of a Lutheran college put it, "angel days of never-ending sabbaticals."

"You'll have regrets," Edward said on my declaring that I intended to stop writing. Regrets humanize. Without regrets people would lack consciences. They wouldn't ponder what might or should have been.

The "could be's" of social and personal reformations wouldn't occur. Certainly, I'll have regrets. Escaping regret is impossible for people of a certain age. The travails of friends and family cause an enervating melancholy pensiveness. Little in life is completely straightforward, however. Contrary to expectation, dark often awakens the imagination more effectively than light. Rather than succumbing to grief or spleen, many people recall, indeed unearth, earlier, gayer times. "Every attic counts old love-letters among its treasures," Myrtle Reed wrote, "and when the rain beats on the roof and grey swirls of water are blown against the pane, one may sit among old trunks and boxes and bring to light the loves of days gone by."

My mind is an attic. Years swell and spring the locks of trunks. Armoires tilt, and clothes bags fall and split. From splay sided boxes memories spill like leaves and sifting across floorboards, sweep through dust, catching on loose nails and the hooks of rusty associations. Not long ago on the attic stairs I found a photograph of me and Alice, my unkissed elementary school girl friend. Alice and I were King and Queen of our sixth-grade class. In the picture I wore a white suit and white buck shoes. Puberty had yet to knock up my cheekbones and stretch my arms and legs. I was soft and muscle-less, and I stared at the camera as I was, a boy uneasy in the headlights of a photographer's studio lamps. Alice stood beside me, her left arm looped through my right. She wore Mary Janes and a high-waisted white dress with a taffeta skirt and a silk belt binding the middle. She was my age but not so ill at ease. She had a knowing and unknowing sweet little girl's expression on her face.

The picture was a remnant of a lost time and place. From the sentimental perspective of Now it seems a remote and lovely Shangri-La. Years ago I threw away sixty newspaper slicks. All were framed and depicted the young me: standing with elementary school classmates, posed at formal high school dances, a nice person beside me, and playing, or attempting to play, sports, a couple of the shots showing me being knocked out of the way by runners crossing goal lines. I cannot explain not keeping the pictures, and now that time is more on my hands than it has been for sixty years, I wish I had them. Whatever motivated me, perhaps something as ordinary as DNA, ridding myself of the pictures was the beginning of a pattern. I've never kept an article or review I wrote. The same goes for interviews with or articles about me. When I received tapes or disks on which I appeared I buried them in the trash. "You have always distrusted the ego," Josh once said, "an inconsistency, remarkable for a person who's spent his adult life writing familiar essays meticulously describing the appointments of his thoughts and days."

Perhaps I was an unacknowledged bye-blow of Thoreau and longed for simplicity. A literary friend once called me "the master of the short declarative sentence." Maybe I succumbed to the delusion that I could control my days. Certainly, I avoided complexity and complex sentences. I loved Nashville and the incomparably dear friends of my youth. But I was too comfortable. Years ago, I mulled writing an autobiography entitled "The Boy Who Ran Away From Life In Order To Have A Life." Writing the book would have obliged me to scrape the surface of things. I would have dug into people's intimate lives, not sexual lives, but the furnishings of their houses and minds. Unknowingly I might have bruised friends, and I could not risk doing that. No matter the selling price, no page is worth causing heartache.

In his poem "Singing Dixie," Neal Bowers begins by reminiscing about old times impossible to forget. He celebrates the ribbon-like beautiful ties of buttercups, peonies, sparrows roosting on a dark afternoon, and dogwood white with blossoms. The final line of the poem "Look away. Look away" echoes "Dixie." The words are not festive, however. They are an imperative exhorting, urging change. Neal is my age and grew up in Clarksville, thirty miles from Nashville. In the 1950s and 60s, and sadly even now, there was much to unlearn and to get away from. Neal has spent most of his life in Iowa and I, in New England. Our relationship with the South has been like a rubber band pulled and released, then pulled and released. I have regrets, but I no longer want to write about the past. I won't cease envisioning fields weedy with redbud and cedar. I'll still see burley growing down the hill behind Grandpa Pickering's house in Carthage. In spring I'll smell the fragrance of magnolias on Grandpa Ratcliffe's farm. In summer an orchestra of cicadas will entertain me, and I'll remember when I wore short pants and was "second locust catcher." I'll recall these and many more, but I won't write about them.

I have reached the time of life when napping in my study not thinking about pages is enough, particularly if Vicki wakes me and hands me a couple of dark chocolate coconut clusters. Many nights I will flutter into the web of Netflix. I'll hang unthinking amid the viscid threads of cheapjack films. Certainly, I will read. For the past two years the university library was closed. As a result, my reading changed, and I purchased used books. All were novels, and most were published before 1920. As I am no longer shiny and bright, so I avoided first editions. Instead, I bought volumes that were battered and warty, books that had felt many hands and were decorated with stains that looked like senile bruises. Their spines suffered from scoliosis, and signatures of pages were herniated. The tales they told differed from those discussed in undergraduate classrooms. Endings were cheery, and none of the stories described people unhappy in exaggerated and supposedly meaningful ways. "Leave digging up pithy elucidation to the young. The old should imbibe the assuaging nectar of boredom," Josh once wrote. "They don't have either the vigor or the inclination to wallow through pages of festering discontent. They should become literary colliers and explore seams of escapist happiness."

If Josh's recipe for octogenarian reading sounds unappealingly lowbrow, so be it. Josh is my age. "Let the energetic and ardent embrace the highbrow," he continued. "Living has bent the shoulders of the aged. Better for them to abjure the funereal tenor of daily life and delight in improbable The Ends." Josh's detractors think his remarks eristic. I am not among his critics, however. On my bedside table is George Barr McCutcheon's *A Fool And His Money*. Published in 1913, the book is a romance. The hero was an occasional novelist who at thirty-five was unattached and testified, "so far as I can tell, unloved." Left a fortune by his Uncle Rilas, he spent little until on a trip to Austria, he noticed an ancient castle perched on "a stupendous crag overhanging" the Danube. Just the place to cuddle the muse, he thought, and on a whim which friends deemed madness, he bought the castle. Then after setting about repairing the battlements, he sensed a plot breaking out, and started a new novel. I haven't read much of the book, and "the girl" hasn't appeared. But she will. She'll have silky brown hair, the neck of a swan, cherry-red lips, skin whiter than porcelain, and mesmerizing eyes, probably brown but maybe sparkling pools of blue. She'll be spirited and as such won't be willowy. She'll probably be five and a half feet tall, the height of bouncy high school cheerleaders in my salad days. After a bump or two, a delicious marriage will be in the offing and at the conclusion. It is unlikely her conversation will resemble that of Benna who lived across the hall from Gerard Maines in Lorrie Moore's *Anagrams* and "who four minutes into any conversation managed to say the word *penis*."

Lives change, but as story-tellers age on the page they fall into patterns and become tedious and repetitious. Years are multipliers. They transform the once-told tale into the often written. Sometimes a writer attempts to rehabilitate a story by slapping a fresh coat of words over it, but he doesn't succeed. The narrative frame remains the same. Last month my friend John called from Tennessee. At Christmas I'd sent him copies of my two most recent books. Before mailing them, I wrote him and mentioning the titles asked if he'd read either of them. On his assuring me that he had not, I inscribed the title pages and mailed the books. "Darn," John recounted in his phone call. "The initial hundred pages of *The World Was My Garden, Too* seemed terribly familiar. I worried that your memory was failing, and you had begun to write the same thing again and again." Although Dementia was rattling my front gate, it had not sprung the lock, or, as Vicki phrases it, I haven't gone bonkerwillie "quite yet." Three years ago, I'd sent John *The World*. He read it. After which he wrote me an appreciative letter— facts which both he and I had forgotten. In the conversation John asked if he could give one of the copies to a friend, a retired pediatrician. "By all means," I said. "As our lives come full circle, we'll need him."

Memory, of course, fails, and for a scribbler to avoid repetition without laying his pen aside is impossible. Words keep reappearing. In February a stranger wrote and said he wanted to open a "conversation" about education. "Thank you for the email," I replied, "but I am too old to start a new correspondence. Indeed, I am too old to continue correspondences that have run for years." That night I realized the exchange echoed one with E.B. White that occurred four decades ago. White was eighty as I am now. I invited him to comment on an aspect of *Charlotte's Web*. Although briefer, two words to my twenty-eight, White's answer resembled my response to my email correspondent. "Too old," White wrote.

"I was the Dreamer, they the Dream," Wordsworth wrote in *The Prelude*, recalling his first sight of Cambridge and its spectacle of gowns, "doctors, students, streets, courts, cloisters, flocks of churches, gateways," and towers. My first sight was of the railway station and a bed-sitter in a boarding house on nearby Station Road where I lived for a year. Beyond the brick wall outside my window loomed a mountain of coal, fuel aplenty for a rich life, a landscape very different from that Wordsworth saw but one that never made me feel I was "not for that hour, nor for that place." I remain comfortable in life, part of the ease coming from the repetitive thoughts and memories of age, the material not awakening enough for a prelude nor for a scribbled conclusion. "Lordy," David wrote me last week, "do I miss our daily romps around the track." Once a nationally ranked runner, David is house bound. I expect that soon I, too, will spend most of my days inside, not simply no more running, but no more mowing, raking and blowing, no more picking up sticks or brewing compost, and no more shoveling and damning the cold.

Essayists write about what they bump against and what bumps against them. Once I fled tranquility and wandered strange deserts of thought and place. Now my life and thoughts are too mundane for even weary readers. I can dress my days so they look like Harlequin, but beneath the costume they will remain the ordinary sentences of erasable paragraphs. Last Tuesday after walking the dogs to the library and back, Vicki and I went on a mall safari. At Munson's Vicki bought a box of chocolate turtles. We stopped at two groceries, Price Chopper in Storrs where I bought a one-dollar lottery ticket and Trader Joe's in Manchester. While Vicki prowled the aisles searching for an Almond Danish Pastry and sundry heart-plugging cheeses, I surreptitiously purchased a two-and-a-half-ounce packet of Trader Joe's Dark Chocolate Covered Almonds. Telling Vicki that I was tired, I fled to the anonymity of the car and ate the almonds, two servings or three hundred and sixty calories worth. Before the excursion Vicki decided I needed new shoes, stability-enhancers, a pair of lightweight boots with thick treads for woods walking and a water repellent town shoe, a hybrid, low on the ankle but with a maze of treads to keep me from sliding off ice and falling into a broken arm. I did not believe I needed new shoes, but Vicki was insistent, and I have aged into the inability to resist well-intentioned bullying. At Skechers I locked my old shoes to the floor and stood steady, but at DSW my resolve collapsed, and I bought the two pairs. From DSW we drove to Panera for lunch. I was exhausted and ate a toasted steak and white cheddar cheese sandwich and a citrus Asian crunch salad with chicken. I supplemented "the mains" with a packet of potato chips and washed everything down with coffee, a light roast for my health.

In the mail at home was a letter from the pediatrician thanking me for the book and a message on the telephone urging me to enroll in a health plan that once a month dispatched a nurse to my house to scrutinize and monitor the medications I took. On the computer was an email from my high school friend Carl informing me that he and Barbara his wife were moving into a CCRC in Minneapolis, that is, a continued care retirement community. "What are you going to do?" he asked. I almost replied that I didn't need to do a goddamn thing because I'd just bought two new pairs of shoes. Actually I'd studied the brochure of an assisted living complex in Bloomfield. I did not tell Vicki, and I have since thrown the brochure away. Because Vicki is twelve years younger than me, I expect she will outlive me. Then the problem of a long life will be hers alone. At the end of his note Carl asked if I were still writing. "No, Hell, no," I wrote and emending MacGrath said, "I've made all the points I ever imagined making and some I shouldn't have made. My writing days are over." I then kicked off my shoes, put on carpet slippers, and settling into the armchair in the television room began reading a tattered novel. "It was not every day that a man could, at one and the same time, fall out of a boat and into the presence of a princess of royal blood," the narrator began. "No siree, bobtail," I thought, "no siree, not every day, only occasionally."

Vicki insists that I explain the title of this book "in a footnote at least." In "California Christmas," I described The Truth's initial appearance. However, I am not a skilled midwife. Once the title squalled and kicked its messy way onto the page, I ignored it. In part I resemble the countryman who said, "Sometimes I tells the truth, and sometimes I doesn't." There are not many absolutes in life. But I suppose that mostly I don't know the truth, or care. I think I agree with a character in Myrtle Reed's *Old Rose and Silver.* "It seems to take a lifetime to learn that wisdom consists largely in a graceful acceptance of things that do not immediately concern us." But whether I agree or disagree winter is ending. Last week the snow melted, and forests opened like fans. Suddenly "Easter Trees" were noticeable, beech saplings to which the old year's leaves clung and rolled into waffle cones, in the sunshine sometimes vanilla, other times wheaten, but always sacral sights.

This morning Vicki walked to the post office without full "parkatation" and double headgear. In town she bought two bouquets of pink oriental lilies. On the way home she stopped at the drugstore and filled a prescription so I could experience a couple of months more of old age. During her absence, I spotted Becky the groundhog lying in the middle of the road. A car smashed her head. Before Vicki returned and noticed Becky, I hurried down the street, picked Becky up, and bringing her home buried her in the wood behind our house. As I rested on my shovel, a flock of Canada geese flew overhead honking, and a titmouse whistled taps. "Natural accompaniments to the burial of animal dead," I thought. "Earth to earth, fur to fur, dust to dust. Would that Beauty were a flower that always lost its petals naturally." Early in the afternoon Erica sent a video of Sammy astride his blue plastic rocking horse galloping across the living room. My elementary school classmate Raymond wrote and told me that our old friends no longer called him "Bird Dog," just "Dawg." After dinner Edward telephoned and asked me to recommend a book to read. "The Truth knows. The Truth has read every dime novel written," Edward said. "Many, but not all," I thought. On the floor in the study was a romance published in 1900. The Truth probably won't read the book. He bought it only because the dedication made his heart skip: "To The Memory Of That Good Friend And Comrade Of My Youth, My Father." The Truth knows the novel's original owner "Miss Helen A. Milne" of "20 Broad Street, Hudson, Mass." purchased it for the same misty-eyed reason.

# About the Author

Sam Pickering isn't bright-eyed, bushy-tailed, and naïve. His world, and pages, however, are green with life. In this collection of essays, he celebrates friendships and the memories of friendships. He rummages through closets of books, some so worm-eaten they are wondrously nourishing. He cures aches and pains by turning them into words. He meanders days and places and looking closely at life finds it intriguing. Under his pen, the imagination soars and the familiar becomes richly appealing, at once both familiar and unfamiliar. He is not a self-help writer, but his essays lighten one's steps and make a person, even a vegan, want to eat a Montreal Sausage and cheer villains, and heroes, at a country wrestling match. Although Sam Pickering lives in Connecticut, he has long been a member of the Fellowship of Southern Writers.

www.ingramcontent.com/pod-product-compliance
Lightning Source LLC
Chambersburg PA
CBHW011758010726
47497CB00013B/3262